W9-AVW-859

Shawnee Books
Also available in this series . . .

The Next New Madrid Earthquake: A Survival Guide for the Midwest
WILLIAM ATKINSON

Vicarious Thrills: A Championship Season of High School Basketball
PAUL E. BATES

Foothold on a Hillside: Memories of a Southern Illinoisan
CHARLESS CARAWAY

Growing Up in a Land Called Egypt: A Southern Illinois Family Biography
CLEO CARAWAY

Vernacular Architecture in Southern Illinois: The Ethnic Heritage
JOHN M. COGGESHALL AND JO ANNE NAST

The Flag on the Hilltop
MARY TRACY EARLE

A Penny's Worth of Minced Ham: Another Look at the Great Depression
ROBERT J. HASTINGS

Southern Illinois Coal: A Portfolio
C. WILLIAM HORRELL

Always of Home: A Southern Illinois Childhood
EDGAR ALLEN IMHOFF

The Music Came First: The Memoirs of Theodore Paschedag
THEODORE PASCHEDAG
AS TOLD TO THOMAS J. HATTON

Escape Betwixt Two Suns: A True Tale of the Underground Railroad in Illinois
CAROL PIRTLE

Heartland Blacksmiths: Conversations at the Forge
RICHARD REICHELT

Fishing Southern Illinois
ART REID

All Anybody Ever Wanted of Me Was to Work: The Memoirs of Edith Bradley Rendleman
EDITH BRADLEY RENDLEMAN
EDITED BY JANE ADAMS

Giant City State Park and the Civilian Conservation Corps: A History in Words and Pictures
KAY RIPPELMEYER-TIPPY

A Southern Illinois Album: Farm Security Administration Photographs, 1936–1943
HERBERT K. RUSSELL

Yankin' and Liftin' Their Whole Lives: A Mississippi River Commercial Fisherman
RICHARD YOUNKER

A Nickel's Worth
of Skim Milk

A Boy's View of the Great Depression

Robert J. Hastings

With a New Preface by the Author

Southern Illinois University Press
CARBONDALE AND EDWARDSVILLE

Copyright © 1972 by the Board of Trustees, Southern Illinois
    University
New preface copyright © 1986 by the Board of Trustees,
    Southern Illinois University
All rights reserved
Printed in the United States of America
Designed by A. B. Mifflin
Illustrated by Steve Kerr

12 11 10 09   10 9 8 7

Library of Congress Cataloging-in-Publication Data

Hastings, Robert J.
  A nickel's worth of skim milk.

  (Shawnee books)
  Reprint. Originally published: Carbondale : University
Graphics and Publications, Southern Illinois University,
1972
  1. United States—social life and customs—1918–1945.
2. Depressions—1929—United States. 3. Hastings,
Robert J.—Childhood and youth. I. Title. II. Series.
E169.H315 1986   973.916   85-30395
ISBN 0-8093-1305-7

To my parents:

GEORGE ELDON HASTINGS
March 17, 1881—May 13, 1968

RUBY BELLE GORDON HASTINGS
June 21, 1893—September 20, 1970

"Southern Illinois is a little south of prosperity."

BAKER BROWNELL, *The Other Illinois*

Contents

Preface

WHEN my mother's body was lying in state at the Mitchell Funeral Home in Marion, Illinois, on September 21, 1970, my eyes were drawn to her hands as well as to her face. Looking at her, I thought too of my father, who had died in 1968. I thought of them, and of their hands, and in that instant their hands became for me symbols of the Great Depression. My parents, like millions of others, had sacrificed and made do with little or nothing. Suddenly, in my eyes, they became heroes, survivors of a great era of American history. They were heroes because they faced the 1930s head on and lived to tell the story.

I decided then to write down some memories of those years to share with relatives. As I reviewed old photographs and clippings, I became more determined. However, I had no idea of writing a book.

In early 1971 I showed the manuscript to my neighbor, Southern Illinois University professor Howard R. Long. He greeted me the next morning, "Bob, you kept me up last night. I read every word. This should be published for anyone to read." So in September of 1972, Southern Illinois University Graphics published *A Nickel's Worth of Skim Milk,* designed by A. B. Mifflin.

Reader response was immediate. People started writing me from all over the country. And all said much the same: "You were writing about my family, as much as your own. That's how I remember the 1930s, too." I soon realized my simple story had struck the heart-strings of thousands of readers. My book was a mirror, as well as a story. These letters were so precious that I deposited them with the Illinois State Historical Library in Springfield. I could not bring myself to destroy a single one.

I was pleased when Southern Illinois University Press decided to reprint this paperback edition. Simultaneously, the Press is publishing a sequel, *A Penny's Worth of Minced Ham.*

(The Depression's getting worse—I started with a nickel, ended with a penny!). These books are the first in the Press's regional series, Shawnee Books. *A Penny's Worth* is also written against the backdrop of the Great Depression. Filled with stories about neighborhood grocery stores of the 1930's, it's saturated with nostalgia and local color.

There is one major difference in the two books. *A Penny's Worth* is illustrated with actual photographs of the Hastings family, our home at 1404 North State in Marion, and grocery stores typical of that era.

One of the photos from the new book is reproduced in this one as well. It's a photograph of a Hastings reunion, made in 1912 in front of our Marion home. I call it my "magic" picture, because the house itself as well as the twenty-nine relatives standing in front of it became the taproot for *A Nickel's Worth* and *A Penny's Worth*.

Although my relatives posed for the magic picture eighteen years before the 1930s, an understanding of who those people were and the history of the house itself will prepare you for the unfolding stories in both books. So before reading further, go back with me to a spring day in 1912 and look deeply into the faces of the twenty-nine people in the photograph.

First, the house. Hezzie Davis bult it in 1905, which means it was just seven years old at the time. Initially, the house had four rooms, a front porch, and a side porch on the south. The side porch was built around a cistern. In 1910, my grandparents, seated in the photo, moved here and enclosed the side porch, making it into another bedroom.

My parents moved here in 1917 and made it their home for forty-three years. I was born here in 1924. They raised the house and put it on a concrete block foundation. The porch, shown here with two steps, had four or five steps when I was a boy.

The house as you look at it faces the east. To your right, or just north of the house, Dad built a one-room neighborhood grocery store, which he operated in the 1920s. That store figures prominently in *A Penny's Worth*.

Now for the people in the photograph.

Seated in front are John Hise and Edie Groves Hastings, my grandparents, who had moved here two years earlier. On this occasion—perhaps an anniversary or a birthday—they were entertaining all of their children except one son, as well as grandchildren and at least one great-grandchild. Notice how two of

Hastings family reunion at 1404 North State Street, Marion, Illinois, 1912.

the sons, Dial and Delmos, far right, are proudly dressed in swallow-tailed coats.

My grandfather was born in Tennessee on January 12, 1846, probably in Smith County. His parents, Robert and Susan Hastings, moved to Kentucky when John was just a boy. While in Kentucky, Susan gave birth to a girl whom they named Tennessee, maybe out of nostalgia or homesickness. By 1860, we find them in Illinois, settled in Williamson County. When the Civil War broke out, John as well as his brother William enlisted in the Union army and saw action in their home state of Tennessee.

After the war, John married Edie Groves and they settled on a farm east of Marion where their children, including my father, were born. All were grown by the time they moved to Marion in 1910.

Several of the men in the photo, including Dad, were miners. It was a dangerous way to earn a living. Two years after this photo was made, Dial Hastings, second from the right on the back row, was burned to death in a powder explosion at Scranton Mine. The date was March 6, 1914. One of his daughters, Flossie, the teenager standing to the back and side of my grandmother, married Ted Boles. Although Ted did not die in an accident, his death was hastened by emphysema and black lung disease, caused by long years in the mines. Flossie's sister, Elva, the teenager standing third from the left in the middle row, married Archie Rodd. A rock fall in a mine broke one of Archie's legs in 1937. A few years later, another rock fall crushed him to death.

My mother, the prettiest woman in the picture, is second from the left. Two of her sisters had already lost husbands in mine accidents. They were John Albright and Marshall Jack, who had married her sisters, Mattie and Bertha.

How do I know the photo was made in 1912? Dad, the second man from the left, is holding my sister, Afton Margaret. Afton was born in 1910 and she appears to be two years old. Also my mother, who appears slightly pregnant, gave birth to her first son, Gordon Champ, in November of 1912.

The older couple who barely got in the photo are an interesting pair. Notice the nattily dressed gentleman on the far left, wearing the white bow tie. And can you make out his wife, who is looking through the "Christmas" window? They are Vardamin and Dialtha Groves James. I often wondered why they didn't want in the picture. Then I concluded they are the only persons who are not of the immediate Hastings family. A sister of my grandmother, Dialtha, was curious and wanted to watch the photographer set up his equipment. She didn't plan to, but she got in the picture anyway. I'm glad she did, for she's the angel who saved our home in the early 1930s. In the photo, she appears to wear a prophetic look on her face—or am I reading that back into it?

One summer about 1931, I was playing in the front yard, just where you see my four cousins sitting on the ground in the photo. I saw Dad coming down the sidewalk, a spring in his step. He was so happy, so light-hearted. He acted twenty years younger than he was.

Here's why. At the time, our home was mortgaged with the Marion Building and Loan for $1,250. Since so many home-owners had defaulted, this company offered to discount their loans drastically, in a desperate effort to keep their own doors open. They offered to settle our mortgage for ten cents on the dollar. That meant if Dad could find $125, the house would be ours, clear and free.

A bonanza—to pay off your mortgage at only one-tenth of its face value? Yes and no. Yes, if you had the $125. But where does an unemployed coal miner find $125 in 1931?

Mr. James, then deceased, was a veteran of the Spanish-American War. Dialtha James, Dad's aunt, received a small government pension. Dialtha lived a simple life and managed well. She was the only relative known to have "a little money."

So she loaned Dad the $125. Earlier on that magic day, he had walked over to her house on North Fair Street a couple of times. Then one or two trips to town, on foot, to the loan company and the courthouse, to see that all the transactions were properly registered. Then home to tell us the house was saved—it was ours! No wonder the sidewalk seemed as light and cushiony as air!

I knew Dad for forty-four years, but I never remember a day when he showed more elation. It is a beautiful memory, one I will cherish always.

And to think that he told me the good news on our front lawn, the very spot where we also saw the Christmas lights about 1935. You see now why I call this 1912 photograph my "magic picture."

I could go on, sharing other memories of that house. But I

must stop and let you get on with the story in both books. The two volumes go together, much like corn bread and skim milk, or minced ham and milk gravy! And always standing in the background, furnishing the inspiration, are the twenty-nine relatives and the ground on which they stood, now almost seventy-five years ago.

I'm indebted to Kenney Withers, director of Southern Illinois University Press, for his conviction that *A Nickel's Worth* deserved reprinting in this edition—and to all his staff for assistance in putting together its younger brother, *A Penny's Worth*.

Preface to the First Edition

FOLLOWING the death of my mother in 1970, I discovered a great number of old letters, newspaper clippings, obituaries and photographs among her personal effects. These unleashed such a flood of memories that I determined to put some of my recollections in writing.

As the project grew, I decided to limit it to the years 1930–38, when I was in grade school in Marion, Illinois, a town with a population of nine thousand, located about 120 miles southeast of St. Louis and 90 miles southwest of Evansville, Indiana. Since these were also the years of the Great Depression, I remember my childhood against that backdrop.

I wanted to write, not from the perspective of a forty-six-year-old adult, but as a grade-school boy; so I have tried to record events as they impressed me at the time. It may seem that too much space is given to food, clothing, housing, jobs and money. But these were important in the thirties, and I cannot erase the role they played in my thinking.

I was the youngest of four children. My only sister, Afton Margaret, moved to St. Louis to work at the Brown Shoe Company when she was sixteen and I was two. Gordon Champ, my oldest brother, left home when I was about seven to work in Chicago, and my youngest brother, Dial LaVerne, joined my sister in St. Louis when I was about nine. So at the time of this story our family included only Mom, Dad, and me.

There was twelve years' difference in my parents' ages. When my story begins, in 1930, Dad was 49 and Mom was 37. When it ends, in 1938, he was 57 and she was 45. Since they were older than many parents of children my age, I was probably exposed to a more mature outlook.

While I have not verified the accuracy of every memory, I did check most names, dates, and places against newspaper clippings, my boyhood diary, old correspondence, and interviews with friends and relatives. If some details are not exactly as others may recall them, remember that these are the impressions of a youngster. Some conditions may have been different, but this is how they impressed me.

Especially helpful was Mrs. William (Lucille Davis) Russell of Granite City, Illinois, whose parents, Ezra and Lizzie Davis, were longtime neighbors—Lizzie being the "walking newspaper" referred to later.

Information on my grandfather's role in the Civil War came from the Report of the *Illinois Adjutant General*, Volume 4, page 187.

Bloody Williamson, by Paul M. Angle (New York: Alfred A. Knopf, 1962), provided interesting details about the violence in my home county from 1922–30.

From the Crash to the Blitz, by Cabell Phillips (New York: The Macmillan Co., 1969), with its amazing variety of photographs and stories from the 1929–39 files of *The New York Times*, helped sharpen my memory.

The Other Illinois, by Baker Brownell (New York: Van Rees Press, 1958), was especially helpful in providing information on the mine wars of Southern Illinois from 1890 to about 1920, which helps explain the plight of the miners in the 1930's.

In a pictorial series published by Time-Life Books of New York, *This Fabulous Century*, I found Volume IV, which covers 1930–40, to be most helpful.

I am also indebted to "A History of the First Baptist Church of Marion, Illinois" by Lee H. Swope, published in booklet form by the church in 1965.

Last, I must acknowledge a unique study by the Works Progress Administration (WPA) of Saline, Williamson, and Franklin counties in Illinois. The title is *Seven Stranded Coal Towns: A Study of an American Depressed Area;* it was written by Malcolm Brown and John N. Webb and published by the Government Printing Office, Washington, D.C., in 1941.

Carbondale, Illinois
March, 1971

A Nickel's Worth of Skim Milk

A Nickel's Worth of Skim Milk

A LOW, sullen yellow cloud had been threatening northeast Marion for nearly an hour. It was May 1, 1930, a prematurely warm day. Many of the neighbor women, who could recall the devastating hailstorm of 1918, were calling their children, closing windows, penning up baby chicks, taking wash off the lines, and debating whether to go to a neighbor's or risk the storm alone.

On one side of the ninety-foot lot at 1404 North State where our home stood, Dad had built a neighborhood grocery in the 1920's, and in 1930 Mom kept the store while Dad worked in the mines. Next door, at 1400 State, stood the big, rambling, two-story Victorian frame home of an older couple, Mr. and Mrs. George Hunter. Mrs. Hunter kept calling to Mom to bring me and my grand-

1

mother, Sarah Gordon, who was visiting us. (I was not quite six, and would not enter school until the fall.)

Mom hesitated because the "bread man" with his bakery truck was due, with fresh loaves to exchange for our day-old bread—some of it the "twin loaves" popular then—and she wanted to pay him the difference. Finally he came, hurriedly made his delivery, and spun his tires as he headed out of our driveway down the Spillertown hard road, hoping to outrun the cloud. We learned later that he was caught by the hail and had to crawl under his truck for safety when the hail beat through the canvas top.

Mom had already closed up the house, and as soon as the bread was delivered she locked the store and we ran to the Hunters'—and none too soon! We were barely inside, standing in a small entry at the bottom of the stairs, when the hailstorm hit. There was little wind, and practically no thunder or lightning. Just darkness and the roar of ice tearing into the shingle roof and shattering the windows.

The elderly Mr. Hunter sat in a rocking chair next to a north window of the living room, holding an old quilt against the pane in an effort to keep the hail out. Around him the other windows gave way, and water poured in, cascading down the staircase to where the rest of us huddled.

"George, let the window go. You'll get cut. Come over here. George! George . . ." But George held his ground, even though he finally lost the battle as the window he was trying to save gave way.

Suddenly the storm was over, and the sun broke through. When we forced open the front door against the hailstones that had piled up on the porch, we beheld an unbelievable sight. What had been just a few minutes earlier a spring day with green grass, trees in full foliage, and lettuce and radishes growing in the gardens, was now the most beautiful winter scene imaginable! The trees, completely stripped, stood naked against the sky as in January. White, glistening hailstones covered the ground like new-fallen snow.

Windows were smashed; big, gaping holes yawned from the rooftops. And as the hail melted, fresh water poured in. The Hunter house was so badly damaged that it was torn down and never rebuilt. Our house needed a new roof, some windows, and wallpaper. After a quick survey of the damage, grandmother Gordon, who had prayed aloud during the storm, quietly gathered hailstones from the back porch and made herself a cup of ice water.

I never forgot the picture of the feeble hands of old Mr. Hunter trying to save a single window from the furious storm. It has become to me a symbol of the heartbreaking efforts of millions of Americans, young and old, who in the next eight years would be trying to weather another storm, the Great Depression. In 1930 Marion, along with the rest of the nation, was reeling from the first onslaught of the worst economic debacle in Western memory—certainly the worst in the history of the United States.

October 24, 1929, was the infamous day of the stock market crash on Wall Street in New York City. Desperate speculators sold 16.4 million shares in one day, and the market plunged $32 billion in value. By the end of 1929, investors had lost $40 billion. By 1931, 2,298 banks had closed. Factories shut down, stores closed, and empty trains ran between once-busy cities where hardly a wisp of smoke now rose in the air. Local governments could collect only a small portion of taxes. Foreign trade came almost to a stop. The number of unemployed Americans rose to six million by the end of 1930, to twelve million in 1931. Before the Depression ended, more than 5,000 banks failed, 32,000 businesses went bankrupt, and unemployment climbed to fifteen million.

Despairing men sold apples on street corners, ate in soup kitchens, and lived in clumps of shacks called "Hoovervilles," named for President Herbert Hoover. Farmers got only a nickel a pound for cotton and less than fifty cents a bushel for wheat. Hourly wages dropped sixty percent, while white-collar salaries fell by forty percent. Hunger was a daily reality. In Chicago, fifty men were seen fighting over a barrel of garbage at the back door of a restaurant.

But this is not my story. I remember the Great Depression as it appeared to a boy living in Marion, a small coal mining town in Southern Illinois. The actions center around our home, just two houses inside the city limits. Here I was born, and here my parents lived from 1918 to 1959.

A NICKEL'S WORTH

I didn't go hungry during the Depression, but some things I did get hungry for. Milk, for instance. I never got enough.

In pre-Depression days, the horse-drawn milk wagon stopped at our door each morning. One of my earliest memories is of bringing in a bottle of icy milk one cold morning. As the milk had frozen and expanded, it had pushed its way out the top, dislodging the little round cardboard cap. I set it on the kitchen stove to thaw. Instead, the heat broke the bottle, and the milk ran popping and spurting across the hot surface.

But the milkman didn't stop during the thirties. Occasionally we would buy a bucket of milk from a nearby farmer, or Mom's sisters from Johnson County would bring us a jugful. For cooking Mom used Pet Milk. It was cheaper than fresh milk and could be kept in summer without refrigeration.

I didn't mind the evaporated milk taste on oatmeal or in cocoa, but I couldn't stomach it on cold cereal. I would try to eat it on my Post Toasties, but the sweet, cooked taste almost turned my stomach, and I would leave the bowl of cereal half eaten. The government surplus powdered milk which we sometimes got from the county relief office was still worse.

Rarely did I feel self-pity during the Depression. But one morning on my way to school I broke the tenth Commandment—"thou shalt not covet . . ." I stopped at a friend's house, and while he was getting dressed, I waited in the kitchen. Unwashed dishes still sat on the table where he had eaten breakfast. Big yellow bananas filled a bowl. A package of corn flakes stood nearby. And in all its white, glistening beauty stood almost a quart of fresh, cold milk from the dairy. For a fleeting minute I questioned why there wasn't enough fresh milk for everyone. It didn't seem fair for my friend to have a whole quart left at his plate while that same morning I had gagged on condensed milk and left it uneaten in my bowl.

But one winter the Marion City Dairy made the most fabulous offer that anyone could possibly imagine. For five cents—one nickel—you could come by on Saturday morning and get a whole bucket of skim milk! The size of the bucket didn't matter. Come Saturday morning, Mom sent me off to the dairy, near downtown by the Missouri Pacific tracks. I held our enamel water bucket in one gloved hand and a nickel in the other.

I took my place in the long line. It was unbelievable. When your turn came, regardless of how big your bucket, you held it under the faucet of the big, stainless steel drum while that white river just ran and ran. Occa-

sionally someone's bucket spilled over, but nobody cared. What extravagance! What a bottomless well of white goodness!

We kept our liquid treasure on the back porch, and the fact that it froze over during the night only added to our delight. Dad came home with big sacks of cracklins that winter (cracklins are pork rinds after the fat is cooked off them for lard), and Mom made pans and pans of cracklin' cornbread. We crumbled the cornbread in tall glasses of milk and ate it like breakfast cereal.

So long as that nickel offer stood, each Saturday found me at the dairy with our water bucket. We had real ice cold dairy milk with Post Toasties for breakfast, in hot cocoa for dinner, with cornbread for supper, and over sliced bananas in between. And for good measure, you just drank a big glassful for the heck of it!

Both Mom and Dad grew up on cornbread and milk. Mom's sister Alverta, who lived on a farm in Johnson County, baked a big pan of yellow cornbread every day during the summer, enough for two meals. Half was eaten hot with the noon meal, and the other half, cold, was served for supper. Cornbread and milk—sweet milk or buttermilk—was their standard evening meal.

I would still just as soon crumble a big square of cornbread in a glass of cold milk as sit down to a T-bone steak and a baked potato mounded with sour cream.

One summer I had what Mom called a "puny spell." When I didn't respond to the conventional Dr. Caldwell's Syrup of Pepsin, she took me to our family doctor. Dr. Parmley weighed me, told me to stick out my tongue, asked how old I was, and pinched my belly to see how much fat I had. "Ruby," he said, "this boy's not getting enough milk and butter. I don't think he needs any medicine. Just feed him a little better."

Since we had no refrigerator, Mom decided that I should go to the store once a day, just before suppertime. Each morning she baked a pan of cornbread, and each afternoon about four I set out for Swan's Grocery on East DeYoung Street with seven cents and a pint bottle. Milk was twelve cents a quart or seven cents a pint, if you brought your own bottle. Back home, I'd sit down to a supper consisting mainly of bread, butter, and milk. Strangely, that summer Mom would call me to the supper table early, before Dad came home. Then she would go out and sit in the front porch swing while I ate alone.

Not until years later, looking back, did I realize how much Mom and Dad liked cornbread and sweet milk. Serving me first, and alone, was her way of making sure I drank the whole pint.

OLD WEST SIDE

"How much did they pay today?" Mom asked as Dad came in with his dinner bucket from a day at the Old West Side mine.

"Nothing. Not a dime. The mine is closed. It's all over."

More than anything else, this cryptic conversation told me, as a six year old, that the Depression had hit 1404 N. State. Black Thursday on Wall Street had passed relatively unnoticed, but now Dad's job was gone, and for the next eight years we would not know a steady income or a regular job. In a few days we closed the neighborhood grocery. Already many customers owed us bills they could never pay. We let the stock go down, then used for ourselves what was left. We hardly knew the exact day the store served its last customer.

The closing of the West Side mine, which was about twelve miles north, at West Frankfort, was not unexpected. The mine had been working only a day or two a week, and wages had been paid on a percentage basis. Officials got together whatever amount they claimed they could, and divided it proportionately—one payday fifty cents on the dollar, another sixty cents. And most of that had to be spent at the company store.

So on the final payday, when the mine closed, many employees were bitter, since they got absolutely nothing for their last two weeks of work. Some said the owners had planned all along to cheat the miners out of their last pay. Others felt the company had operated the mine as long as it could, sharing with the miners what little profit there was.

Like many Southern Illinois men, Dad knew little about any trade except mining. On September 28, 1916, he had been issued Illinois Miner's Certificate 17229 in Book 172, after two years' experience and a written exam. The certificate says he was then thirty-five years old, five feet ten-and-a-half inches tall, weighing 135 pounds, and having black hair and grey eyes.

Dad had no ambition to have any of his three sons follow him into the mines. There were few safety regula-

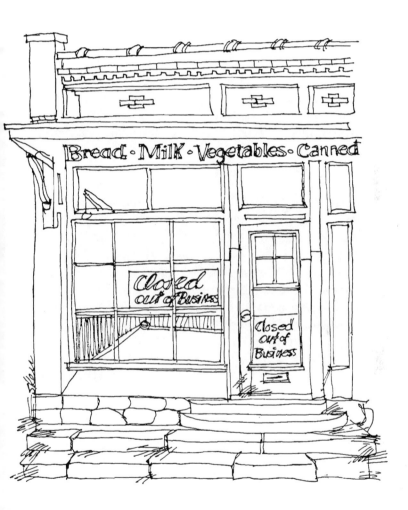

tions. My brother LaVerne did try it for two or three days. On his first day in the pits the hoisting engineer "dropped the cage," a traditional initiation for a new miner. Dad wore a carbide lamp fastened to his mine cap, and its open flame was a constant invitation to a gas explosion.

Southern Illinois mines reached out with their black, grimy hands for three of our relatives. Dial Hastings, Dad's brother, died in a powder explosion at Scranton Mine. Marshall Jack, the first husband of Mom's sister Bertha, died in a mine. And Archie Rodd, who married Dial's daughter, Elva, was crushed to death in a slope mine near Harrisburg.

Dad carried a three-tiered aluminum dinner bucket. The bottom compartment held drinking water, the middle section sandwiches and fruit, and the top part pie or cake. When the miners "threw out their water," it meant they emptied their buckets of drinking water and were ready to go home—maybe because of a lack of "empties" (cars to load), or a dispute of some sort, or because they were feeling good and wanted a day off. Or maybe the mine would "blow over"—sound the whistle—because of a breakdown or to signal one of those too-frequent accidents that crushed out the life of a miner.

I remember looking forward to opening Dad's dinner bucket when he came home, in hopes of finding a chicken leg or a slice of raisin pie. Not that I was all that hungry —but there was always a suggestion of surprise or mystery. He would tell me about standing at the bottom of the shaft and looking up at the sky, and being able in the daytime to see an occasional star because of the darkness in which he stood.

Modern machinery has since replaced the old pickaxes, the shots of powder into the face of the coal, the hand shovels, and the carbide lamps.

Anyone who grew up in Southern Illinois in the 20's and 30's remembers the old shaft mines, most of which have long since given way to giant shovels that strip the dirt from over the coal seams. There was Slogo and New Virginia and Peabody 3, 11, and 18. And Old Gent, Scranton, West Side, Orient 1 and 2, Stiritz, Paulton, Sloppy Hollow and White Ash. And Bell & Zoller 4, Lake Creek 1 and 4, Old Wasson, and Old Ben 8, 9, and 15.

Coal mining had a spectacular growth in Williamson, Saline, and Franklin counties between 1900 and 1925. At their peak, a hundred mines were hoisting coal every day in these three counties; their mine payroll reached $40 million in 1926. Day after day, in 1926, the big New Orient Mine in Franklin County broke the world's record for tonnage hoisted in an eight-hour shift.

Most of the residents in these mining counties were descended from settlers who came between 1870 and 1910 from the West Kentucky hills. In speech and folkways the area was culturally homogeneous with the western Appalachians and distinctly unlike central and northern Illinois. In addition to the Kentuckians, several large foreign-born groups settled in Southern Illinois between 1900 and 1920 because the mines offered them work. These were principally Italians, Hungarians, Croatians and Ukrainians.

Then came the crash. About a hundred mines were abandoned before the Depression was over, with a loss of twenty thousand jobs. Taxpayers stopped paying, and local governments found themselves without funds. In 1930 the school tax collections dropped by one-fourth. The high schools were crowded as boys who would formerly have entered the mines now stayed in school. At the same time, many teachers were laid off, or paid in warrants which were sometimes cashed for fifty cents or less on the dollar.

The federal government identified Saline-Franklin-Williamson as one of fifty distinct depressed areas. These areas received three or four times the WPA unemployment quotas allotted to average communities of a similar size.

Benton, a town of eight thousand residents nineteen miles north of Marion, was forced to turn off its street lights, stop all work on the streets, reduce the fire department personnel to the minimum required by the insurance companies, and cut the police force to one—underpaid—employee.

All the banks in Marion, as well as nearby Creal Springs and Johnston City, went under. Merchants paid their bills with post office money orders or by endorsing checks they received and forwarding them. Some even paid their bills with postage stamps. All told, thirty-four banks in the three counties closed within a two-year period, and $7 million in savings was swept away. The situation was so tight that at one low point the Marion school term was reduced to six months.

A unique feature of the Depression in Williamson County was the emergence of about 150 small, makeshift "gopher holes," where farmers and unemployed miners dug shallow-vein coal for local sale. They would sink a slope about fifty or seventy-five feet deep and mine the poor grade of coal. Most of the loading was done by hand. Many had no storage space at the tipple, and would hoist coal only when someone was waiting to buy a load.

Geologists estimate that 135 to 200 billion tons of coal underlie two-thirds of Illinois—enough coal to last more than a thousand years at the present rate of consumption. Illinois has one of the largest coal reserves in the world; greater than that of Pennsylvania or any other state east of the Mississippi, and greater than those of most nations of the world.

But my boyhood memory of Williamson County is of decaying tipples, silent whistles, smokestacks cold and mute against grey skies.

So although the closing of Old West Side crippled our family, we were not alone. The standstill was area wide.

DIGGING IN

The closing of Old West Side Mine meant the end of anything resembling a steady job for the next eight years. From 1930 on, it was a day's work here and a day's work there, a coal order from the welfare office, a relief check, a few days on WPA, a garden in the back yard, and a few chickens and eggs.

We weathered the storm because of Dad's willingness to take any job and Mom's ability to stretch every available dollar. It was not so much a matter of finding a job as of filling in with odd jobs wherever and whenever you could, and most of the "jobs" were those you made for yourself.

My diary shows that Dad sold iron cords door to door, "worked a day in the hay," bought a horse to break gardens, rented an extra lot for a garden on the shares, picked peaches, raised sweet potato slips, traded an occasional dozen of eggs at the grocery, hung wallpaper, "painted Don Albright's house for $5," picked up a day or two's work at the strip mines, guarded the fence at the county fairgrounds, cut hair for boys in the neighborhood, sold coal orders, and when he had to and could, worked intermittently on WPA.

With no dependable income, we cut back on everything possible. We stopped the evening paper, turned off the city water and cleaned out our well, sold our four-door Model T touring car with the snap-on side curtains and isinglass, stopped ice and milk delivery, and disconnected our gas range for all but the three hot summer months. There was no telephone to disconnect, as we didn't have one to start with!

We did keep up regular payments on two Metropolitan Life Insurance policies. Page after page of old receipt books show entries of 10¢ per week on one policy and 69¢ a month on another. As long as we could, we made house payments to the Marion Building and Loan, but a day came when we had to let those go, too.

Fortunately, we were able to save our house from foreclosure. When so many borrowers defaulted, the Marion Building and Loan went bankrupt. Creditors were allowed to pay just about any amount to satisfy the receivers. But that was the catch—who had "just about any amount" to pay? A house behind ours sold for $25. Many good houses in Marion sold for $5 to $100 and were torn down and moved to nearby towns. We settled with the loan company for $125, or ten cents on the dollar for our $1250 mortgage. I'll never forget the day Dad cleared it all up, making two or three trips to town to bring papers home for Mom to sign. He was able to borrow the $125 from his aunt, Dialtha James, who as the widow of a Spanish-American War veteran had a small pension.

Looking back, I find it amazing what we did without. A partial list would include toothpaste (we used soda), toilet paper (we used the catalog), newspaper or magazine subscriptions, soft drinks, potato chips and snacks, bakery goods except bread and an occasional dozen of doughnuts, paper clips, rubber bands, and restaurant meals. We had no water bill, sewer bill, telephone bill, no car expenses—gasoline, tires, batteries, licenses, insurance, repairs—no laundry service, no dry cleaning (we pressed woolens with a hot iron and a wet cloth), no bank service charge (no bank account), no sales or income tax. We sent no greeting cards except maybe half a dozen at Christmas.

There were no convenience or frozen foods, vitamin tablets, bandaids, kleenex, paper towels. Garbage pickup, TV and TV repairs, long-distance calls, health insurance, Scotch tape—these necessities of today were unknown to us then.

Typical of the simple economies that Mom practiced was keeping the electric bill to $1 a month and the gas bill to $1 a month in June, July, and August. I know, because I rode my bicycle to town to pay these bills.

Since our only appliance was an electric iron, the chief use of electricity was for lighting. With only a single bulb suspended by a cord from the ceiling of each room, there weren't many lights to burn, even if they were all turned on at the same time. But that's the point—they weren't. On winter evenings Mom would turn on the kitchen light while she cooked supper. If I had lessons I brought them to the kitchen table or sprawled on the floor between the kitchen and dining room.

After supper we "turned off the light in the kitchen" and moved to the dining-sitting room, where another light was switched on. If we wanted to read on winter afternoons, we sat as near a window as possible, with the curtains pinned back, to save the lights until it was nearly dark. In the summer we often made our way to bed in the dark, not so much to save a penny or two as to "keep the house cool" and not attract the bugs.

When ironing, Mom saved flat pieces such as towels and handkerchiefs to the last, to be pressed while the iron was cooling and the electricity was off. To save gas in the summer, she planned her meals to make maximum use of the oven, so if she was roasting meat, she would also be baking cookies. Utensils were often stacked two deep on the range so that a boiling pot of beans would help to cook the potatoes.

Dad had some old-fashioned shoe lasts, and he would buy stick-'em-on soles at the dime store to patch our shoes in winter. With simple barber tools he cut my hair and that of other kids in the neighborhood, for maybe ten cents a head. In cold, wet weather when he worked outdoors on WPA he often cut strips of cardboard to stuff in the soles of his shoes and keep his feet warm.

We took care of what we had. Every cotton cloth was used over as a dish cloth, wash cloth, dust cloth, shoe-shining cloth, window-washing cloth, to scrub and wax floors, make bandages, make quilt pieces, make kite tails, or to tie boxes and papers together. The cotton bags from flour, salt, or cracked chicken feed were washed, bleached, and cut into dish cloths and towels. Some neighbors made curtains or even dresses from feed sacks. Every paper bag was saved for lunches or cut and used for wrapping paper. String was wound into balls for later use.

Each August Mom would find someone who was a year ahead of me in school, and buy his used books. One exception was a spelling book used in all eight grades. Since it was to be used for eight years, we decided it would be a wise investment to buy a new one when I started first grade. In the seventh grade, I dropped that speller in the snow. I thought Mom was unfair when she sent me all the way back to school, retracing my steps to look for the book. Fortunately, I found it about two-thirds of the way back.

Sometimes, over a weekend, Mom would count out enough slices of bread to make my lunches for the following week. They would be set aside and used for nothing else. She did the same for Dad's lunch if he happened to be working, as we bought groceries only once a week. If she baked an angel food cake, she saved back enough for lunches each day of the week. She usually wrapped my lunch in newspaper and tied it with a string.

Before the Depression, we hung a four-cornered black-and-white cardboard sign in the front window each morning. The figures in the corners told the iceman how many pounds to bring—25, 50, 75, or 100. But ice was one of the casualties of the Depression, although we managed a small piece two or three times a week for iced tea. About eleven in the morning I would pull a little wagon, filled with a gunny sack and assorted old quilts and tarpaulins, down to the neighborhood ice house to buy "a nickel's worth of ice," which was half of a 25-pound chunk. By wrapping it carefully and storing it in a cool, damp spot under the house, we could stretch that piece of ice for two or three days. In rainy, cool weather, maybe four days! It was our glistening prize, and any left over from tea was emptied back into a pitcher of ice water, or used for lemonade that afternoon. So as not to waste any, we chipped only what was needed, with much of the same care used by a diamond cutter.

Whatever was free was our recreation. This may have included playing records on our wind-up victrola or listening to the Atwater-Kent radio. You might watch a parachute jump at the airport or a free ball game at the city park, with perhaps a free band concert afterwards and the side attraction of a watermelon-eating contest (with your hands tied behind you). The band concerts survived only the first two years of the Depression.

Or you might go out to the airport hangar to watch the dance marathon, cringe at the risks taken by the Dodge-'Em cars at the fairgrounds on Labor Day, or attend a medicine show where the hawker peddled a single elixir said to cure everything from arthritis to zymosis. There were family dinners and picnics, and occasionally four or five families would pile into the back of Ted Boles' coal truck for an overnight camping-fishing trip to the Ohio River at Shawneetown or Metropolis.

We liked music, and one of my earliest memories is of Dad singing to me:

> Two arms that hold me tight,
> Two lips that kiss goodnight;
> To me he'll always be,
> That little boy of mine.
>
> No one can ever know,
> Just what his coming has meant;
> He's something heaven has sent,
> That little boy of mine.

One spring morning he came in and sat on the edge of my bed. I had been sick a few days, but now the sun was shining and he was encouraging me to get up and play. Outside the birds were singing.

"Do you know what the birds are singing?" he asked me.

"No."

"They're singing, 'Bobby get up, Bobby get up . . .'"

When I was small, Dad taught me a ballad that I would sometimes perform for visiting relatives, standing on the footstool as I sang:

> Oh hand me down my walking cane,
> Oh hand me down my walking cane,
> Oh hand me down my walking cane,
> For I'm gonna leave on that midnight train,
> For all my sins are taken away, taken away.

Now if I die in Tennessee,
Now if I die in Tennessee,
Now if I die in Tennessee,
Ship me back by C.O.D.,
For all my sins are taken away, taken away.

The lament continued with several verses: "Oh I got drunk, and I got in jail . . . had no one to go my bail . . . the beans was tough, and the meat was fat . . . come on Momma, and go my bail, get me out of this buggy jail . . . for all my sins are taken away, taken away."

At one point in the Depression, the cupboard was literally bare of money. We weren't hungry, but we were penniless. Then Dad went back in the pantry and came out with a jar in which he had saved a few nickels and dimes for such an emergency.

Later, Mom said to me, "I've learned that whatever happens, your Daddy always has a little dab of money put back somewhere . . ."

SOUR GRAPEFRUIT AND WPA

President Franklin D. Roosevelt's "New Deal" used all twenty-six letters of the alphabet to identify the various government programs aimed at the economic crisis. There were, to name a few, the FERA, CCC, PWA, AAA, NRA ("We do our part"), NYA, and WPA.

Millions of dollars poured into direct welfare, surplus food, and government work projects, known first as the PWA (Public Works Administration) and later as the WPA (Works Progress Administration).

Eventually, eight million men worked on WPA projects during the Depression. In some areas the money was spent on public buildings, schools, bridges, and airports. Around Marion most people felt it was wasted on "make-work" projects, so WPA was nicknamed "We Piddle Around." As I remember, it was road work for the most part—clearing right-of-way and opening up ditches—and a long-handled shovel was the standard tool.

To its credit, the WPA did construct 150,000 toilets. The design was so distinctive that "WPA toilet" still describes the conventional outdoor sanitary privy.

Like thousands of miners and other unemployed men in Southern Illinois, Dad applied for a WPA job. But he didn't like anything about it. He resented every day. He felt that the questionnaires were humiliating and that those who conducted the interviews were rude. When there was no WPA job, and he had to apply for welfare, he felt the same embarrassment. Whether this was his pride, or whether those lucky enough to get political jobs administering the government programs acted uppity, I don't know. Maybe a bit of both.

WPA was intermittent—a few days' work and then a layoff when funds gave out. Top monthly pay was $44, but Dad seldom drew the full amount because of frequent layoffs or bad weather, especially in the winter. When a man was laid off, he was given Form 403, so the most feared news was, "Bill got his 403 today," or, "Henry says they're going to give all of us our 403's on Friday." It was almost like a death sentence.

WPA workers in and around Marion, with their long-handled shovels moving dirt that didn't necessarily need moving, dressed in long overcoats and with mufflers wrapped around their faces and necks—this is one of the indelible images of the Depression. To keep warm in cold, muddy weather, Dad wore two or three pairs of socks and lined the thin bottoms of his shoes with newspaper or cardboard.

Dad was working on WPA in 1936 when my brother LaVerne died. When he went back to work, the men said, "Eldon, if you'd let us know, we'd have given our time and dug the grave." When he told Mom, she said, "I don't want no WPA shovel stuck in my boy's grave."

This was said, not out of ingratitude, but out of a deep pride that believed a mother and father should at least be able to bury their own son.

Welfare, or "relief," as it was known, was also intermittent. Occasionally we might get a "relief order" for groceries or an "order for coal"—these could be redeemed at the store or the mine but not converted into cash.

Then there was the surplus food—canned stew meat, powdered milk, and grapefruit. The powdered milk, unlike that of today, was hopeless. It wouldn't dissolve, but instead formed big lumps. Its taste and odor were beyond description. Mom did manage to use some of it in cooking, but most of it went to the chickens.

I had never tasted grapefruit until Dad brought home a sack from the relief office. I don't even remember hav-

ing seen any in the stores. Everyone thought they were unbearably bitter and sour. Neighbors gave them to us by the peck, saying they were "not fit for a hog to eat." Mom solved the problem by slicing them in half the night before and sprinkling them with sugar, which filtered down into the fruit during the night, and then serving them for breakfast. We didn't throw any away.

We resented the welfare and the WPA, and especially the attitudes of those in Williamson County who administered the programs. At a time when we needed help most, we were made to feel undeserving, lazy, and shiftless. We knew better, but our pride hurt just the same.

DAD'S LETTUCE BED

On the home front we fought the Depression with spades and hoes and rakes and a worn-out garden plot, but the unusually hot and dry summers of the early 30's mocked our efforts. It seemed inevitable in 1933, '34, and '35 that potatoes grew no larger than marbles, tomato vines curled up to die, and cutworms got the bunch beans.

But we came back, summer after summer, setting out not only our own little garden, but often tending garden on the two vacant lots next door. Neighbors had a wonderful way of sharing what they did raise, for everyone put out something. If a neighbor's corn turned out well, he shared "at least a mess" with other families. If you learned that someone raised a good sweet potato crop, you would "speak for a bushel" in late summer.

It was an unwritten law that no one paid for, say, "a mess of beans," but that if you "spoke for" so many bushels or pounds, then you paid.

We kept a keen eye out for anything that was edible. In the spring Mom picked poke greens, wild lettuce, and dandelion greens in the yard and empty lots. We knew that down the Spillertown hardroad was a lone persimmon tree which shared its fruit after the first hard frost. And across the street, Walter Lang's mulberry tree was good for at least one pie. Over on Glendale Street, Ezra Davis had a cherry tree whose fruit he shared with anyone who would pick it.

One summer, according to my diary, Mom canned cucumbers for Mrs. John Wallace on the halves, and I picked her tomatoes one day for a dime. Then she gave me another quarter for taking tomatoes down the street to her mother.

Dad usually got a few days' work in the peach or apple orchards each summer, taking his pay primarily in fruit. He would come home from the big peach orchards down by Anna with his miner's bucket bulging with the choicest and largest Elbertas, Hales, or Yellow Clings.

I never liked working in the garden, maybe because we raised so little the first summers I was old enough to work. On March 14, 1937, I wrote in my diary, "Guess we will have another garden this summer." Then, in red ink, "I don't like to farm."

One reason I must have written "to farm" was that on March 7 of that spring, Dad bought a horse for $40. He hoped to earn that much and more by breaking gardens for other people and by planting an extra plot or two on the shares. But when you realize that $40 was equal to a month's cash income, that horse becomes very expensive. No wonder that on March 9, two days later, I told my diary, "Dad is ready to sell his horse."

With the grape arbor we were more successful. The dry summers didn't seem to affect the Concord grapes, which furnished us with juice, pies, jelly, and even green grape pie, a delicacy much like gooseberry pie, for which the green grapes must be picked within a week of the stage when they are crispest. The vines climbed four posts, which in turn supported a latticework overhead, so the shade of the grape arbor was a cool place to sit. Here Mom would often sew, snap beans, or peel peaches on summer mornings, while Dad would rest here periodically from spading or hoeing.

One of our most successful projects was a hot bed, which Dad made for two or three summers. In this bed made of manure and covered with glass or sheet metal, we raised sweet potato sets, tomato sets, and a few onion sets. The same spring we invested in the horse, Dad sold ten thousand sweet potato slips at twenty cents a hundred, for a total of $20. The next year, 1938, I wrote in my diary that sales were "slow," amounting to only a few hundred slips. But in 1937 it seemed that the mug where Dad kept his change, in the kitchen cabinet, would spill all over everywhere. During the Depression, any extra cash, however small the amount, was looked upon as buried treasure suddenly brought to light.

As a gardener, Dad was best known for his lettuce bed. He planted it early enough to beat the drought and heat, and he was never known to fail. Neighbors came to expect him to raise the best lettuce in the north end of Marion. On summer mornings they would come to our back door, paper sack or dishpan in hand, to buy "a nickel's worth of lettuce for dinner." Or, in rare cases, a dime's worth!

I always knew spring was near when I came home from school on Valentine's Day and found Dad putting the finishing touches on his lettuce bed. Weeks earlier he had spaded it up and covered it with sheets of tin salvaged from the roof of an old barn that had once stood on the back of our lot. This kept the bed dry. Using pieces of screenwire, he had sifted ashes from the heating stove until they were powdery and then mixed them with the dirt. Then he had raked the bed, back and forth, lengthways and sideways and crossways, until the dirt was as smooth as a calm lake on a windless day. Now he was ready to scatter the tiny seeds. If there was snow on the ground, all the better, for seed planted on top of snow would be more evenly distributed when it settled to the ground.

So we raised lettuce for ourselves, our neighbors, our relatives, and even the chickens, because they enjoyed it by the bushel. Once Dad had earned a neighborhood reputation, he kept expanding the lettuce bed until it seemed he grew enough to feed the whole town. In early May, before many people had lettuce in their own gardens, he sold some to the grocers on consignment.

It seemed that we ate lettuce by the ton. A typical spring meal was a big pan of lettuce wilted with hot bacon grease and vinegar, finely chopped and mixed with green onions and tiny radishes. To this we added cornbread, a few strips of bacon, potatoes boiled in their jackets, and iced tea, and we had a real feast.

MOM'S FRIED CHICKEN

One June morning in the summer of 1936, following the death of my brother LaVerne, Mom took her sharpest butcher knife, a teakettle of boiling water, and two shallow pans out to the well. These, plus a couple of buckets of cold water which I drew from the well, were placed on what we called the laundry bench.

Opening a gate made of the same pointed red pickets as the fence, she stepped into the chicken yard. Grabbing the fattest spring fryer, she quickly wrung its neck, and we watched while it flapped and flopped to death in the dust.

She scalded the fryer in the boiling water, plucked and saved the feathers, and then quickly cut the bird into frying pieces. I had watched her do this many times, but today seemed to be different. She rinsed the meat in the cold well water a couple of times more than usual, then repicked the pinfeathers until the chicken was naked as a peeled egg.

Wrapping the meat carefully in waxed paper, she said to me, "Take this to Dr. and Mrs. Johnson's. Go to the back door. And say, 'We want you to accept this in the spirit in which it is given.' "

So with the still-warm fryer under my arm, I rode my bicycle downtown to the parsonage of the First Baptist Church on West Monroe Street. George L. Johnson, our pastor, had preached LaVerne's funeral. On my way, I said my presentation speech over and over.

When Mrs. Johnson answered my knock, I spoke mechanically, like a first grader who has memorized a part in a play. "My mother said for you to accept this chicken in the spirit in which it is given."

I didn't know exactly what that meant, but I learned the next Sunday when Mrs. Johnson stopped me in the hallway at church. "Tell your mother that was the best chicken our family ever tasted," she said.

Without the few chickens we raised, our table would have gone much barer during the Depression. Not only were our chickens a valuable source of food, but they doubled as gifts of friendship, such as to the Johnsons in appreciation for a funeral sermon, or in our annual Christmas box to my sister in St. Louis.

We raised perhaps fifty fryers each spring, and kept about eighteen laying hens and a rooster through the winter. They kept us in eggs, and occasionally, in the spring when they were laying well, we had an extra dozen to sell for 15¢. And a good fryer always brought a dollar during the Depression—one of the few items which is cheaper today than in 1936.

Mom's goal was to serve the first fryer by her birthday, June 21, and we usually made it, though I fear that at times we ate some awfully little fellows. On many a summer day we feasted on tender fried chicken, mashed potatoes, milk gravy, and cole slaw with Mom's own egg-and-vinegar dressing.

Ordinarily, we raised our own chickens. When a hen was ready to "set," we saved setting eggs, and Dad fixed nests in wooden boxes in the smoke house.

But one memorable spring we ordered fifty baby chicks from the Otis Carter Hatchery in nearby Eldorado. In fact, lots of people, not only in Southern Illinois but other states, ordered chickens from Carter's—Otis Carter was a salesman as well as a hatcheryman.

Each spring he sponsored a six A.M. country music program from WEBQ in Harrisburg. Only he didn't drive to the studio in Harrisburg. He broadcast his folksy music and homespun philosophy right from his hatchery in Eldorado—by *remote control!* I italicize "remote control" because it was eight miles from Harrisburg to Eldorado and, although we didn't know the exact meaning of remote control, we knew it was a feat to sing in Eldorado and broadcast from Harrisburg, all at the same time.

As I said, Carter was a salesman. He would hold the microphone right over the incubators, and you could hear the chirping of those little White Leghorns, Plymouth Rocks, New Hampshires, Rhode Island Reds, Wyandottes, and "Domineckers" all over Southern Illinois. He made you think that a few chickens in your back yard

would guarantee happiness and prosperity and make the
Depression seem like a land boom.

Later, Mr. Carter recorded his programs, put them
on WSM in Nashville, Tennessee, and sold chickens
throughout the mid-South. Curtis Small, publisher of
the *Harrisburg Register*, remembers trucks lined up at
the Harrisburg post office, waiting to unload shipments
of chicks going to all parts of the country.

Nothing was wrong with the Carter chicks we ordered
that spring, but something was wrong with the weather.
It was wet and cold. We weren't equipped. In desperation, after "Carter's little chicks" started dying, we
fenced off a little corner of our kitchen and brought them
right in the house. We put newspapers on the floor to
catch the droppings and a horrible-colored medicine in
their water to keep them well, but to no avail. Most of
them died, and every time we lost a chick we felt as if
we were losing a friend. A $1 friend, too. A Sunday din-
ner friend. And scrambled eggs on cold mornings and
colored eggs at Easter.

And I couldn't help feeling a little sick when Dad
picked up one of the little fellows by the feet and pitched
the tiny corpse into the heating stove.

After this experience we returned to letting nature
take its course, encouraging every old hen who thought
she could cut the mustard to raise her own. At least she
could warm them under her wings and scratch in the
grass and cluck excitedly when she found a fat worm.

Since we had chickens, we didn't need a food disposal.
Not a scrap was ever wasted. Everything—even potato
peelings—went into the "chicken pan," which was emptied two or three times a day. We supplemented this
with cracked corn and leftover bread from my Aunt
Bertha's.

Dad took a personal interest in our chickens, often
making pets out of them. I often wondered how he could

take an ax to one of them after petting them like he did. In winter he took warm water to the chicken house to thaw out their frozen drinking pans. He even warmed their scraps on the stove and then squatted down to pet them while they ate. In extreme weather he crumbled in their food a few pods of red pepper, which Mom kept strung near her cookstove. He thought the hot pepper would warm them up. Whether it did or not, they surely sensed the warmth of his affection.

He saved eggshells, warmed them in the oven until they were dry and crisp, and then crumbled them in the chicken feed to add calcium to the diet. And if Dad didn't waste a morsel of their feed, Mom didn't waste even their feet when she cleaned a chicken. (I'm sure many of the present generation have never even seen a chicken foot.)

"My mother cleaned the heads, but I never learned to," she would say as she skinned the gizzard or feet. The "bony pieces"—wings, back, neck, gizzard, liver, and feet—would go for dumplings or chicken soup. The "good pieces" would be fried, and full-grown hens would be baked whole. We had fried chicken, barbecued chicken, boiled chicken, baked chicken, chicken and dressing, chicken and dumplings, ground chicken in sandwiches—you name it, we had it. And the feathers we dried for pillows. About the only waste was the squawk!

Now about that leftover bread from Aunt Bertha's. She baked hot bread twice a day—biscuits for breakfast and cornbread for dinner. Or, if Uncle Charley was working, cornbread for supper. Only she baked about three times as much as they needed. And she was never one to eat a day-old biscuit or warmed-over cornbread.

This she faithfully saved for our chickens, separating the dry bread from other table scraps. About once a week I would stop on my way from school, or even make a special trip, to pick up her leftover bread, saved in meal or flour sacks. I'll bet I carried a ton of old bread from 109 West White to 1404 North State during the Depression. It was about a mile, and sometimes there was more than a week between my stops. In that case, Aunt Bertha would send word by anyone who passed, "Tell Bobby if he doesn't come for this bread, I'm going to burn it up!"

I always would, and she never did.

Maybe it was because she liked Mom's fried chicken as much as we did.

THE GINGERBREAD BOY

"I am a gingerbread boy, I am, I am. I am a gingerbread boy." These were the first words I learned to read.

I remember when I first sensed that printed words have meaning. Dad was sitting in a rocking chair behind the heating stove. I was standing by his side, and we were looking at my first reader. He underlined the words as he said them aloud, "I . . . am . . . a . . . gin . . . ger . . . bread . . . boy."

Grace McDonald was my first grade teacher at the Jefferson School on East Boulevard, and on the Friday afternoon when we completed the gingerbread story, she announced a surprise.

"But first, pick up the scrap paper in the aisle to your right . . . now on your left . . . and now under your seats. The first row finished, with each pupil sitting erect and his hands folded on his desk, may pass to the lunchroom."

We wondered why Miss McDonald would take us to the lunchroom so late in the afternoon. "Lunchroom" was a glorified name for a sparsely furnished room with five or six odd-sized tables and folding chairs, a two-burner gas stove, a doll-sized sink, a counter, and a rickety glass candy case. If you had rounded up a dime for lunch, you could buy a nickel hamburger and a nickel bottle of chocolate milk. The next day you could buy another nickel hamburger and chocolate milk. That was the standard menu, plus a few scraggly boxes of candy in the glass case. Most of us brought our lunches.

As we marched into the lunchroom that afternoon, a real gingerbread cookie, cut in the shape of a boy, sat at each place.

Who had ever dreamed that gingerbread boys really existed? Who dared imagine that a teacher would make enough cookies for every pupil—big, fat, brown gingerbread boys that were ours to eat right then and there!

How to describe the clash of emotions! On the one hand, the desire to eat the cookie. On the other, a wish to make the cookie boy last and last to remind you of the first story you ever read.

If the importance of one cookie seems exaggerated, all I can say is that I can still see the hollow eyes and sunken cheeks of some of those Depression kids. Even I, at six years old, knew some of them were coming to school hungry. Against that backdrop, a whole cookie for each child in the class took on heightened significance. It was a simple gesture. But it was a red-letter day. I'll never forget it.

Floyd Baggett, the principal at Jefferson, doubled also as fifth grade teacher, playground director, disciplinarian, truant officer, and sometimes, I guess, janitor. In the early thirties the school term was cut back to eight months. Even then, the school board sometimes paid with vouchers meant to be redeemed the following summer after taxes were collected. Since most teachers needed their pay to live on, they cashed them at a discount, usually 90¢ on the dollar, to pay their bills. This meant a further cut in real salary.

Mr. Baggett was a father-image to all of us. Although he chewed a little tobacco, he could swing a ball bat like a teenager. He was one of those rare persons who, even in the Depression, seemed to smile when he carried on an ordinary conversation. He radiated hope and enthusiasm, and not only believed the best about tomorrow, but helped you believe it too.

One day he announced, "Now I want all of you to take a plain sheet of notebook paper. Make up a little story of your own. Or a poem. Just so it's yours. Sign your name at the bottom. And pass your papers to the front when you're finished. There's no hurry. Write your story at home tonight, if you wish."

The next day I turned in "The Midnight Raiders." It was a hair-raising poem about a band of ruffians that robbed and beat up a pioneer family, then burned their prairie cabin. I suppose it was in a sense autobiographical, for we dreaded fire at home. It was the enemy that might take our house, our furniture, and our clothing. Since these things were all we had, we treasured them highly.

When the papers came back, my heart sank. Mine had no grade. But at the bottom of the sheet, Mr. Baggett had struck through "By Bobby Hastings."

Instead, he had written, "By Henry W. Longfellow."

This so impressed me that I can still see the bold, swift strokes of his handwriting, and even the dark blue ink of his broad pen.

I knew I was not Henry W. Longfellow. Floyd Baggett knew I was not Longfellow, that famous nineteenth-century American poet who wrote such favorites as "The Song of Hiawatha" and "The Courtship of Miles Standish." But it was his way of saying, "I believe in you."

And if a ten-year-old boy's favorite male teacher believes in him, what else matters?

A DRINK AT HEZZIE'S WELL

In 1905, when Hezzie Davis built a four-room, L-shaped frame house at 1404 North State for his bride, Lea, he dug two wells. A soft-water well, or cistern, was on the side porch, and a hard-water well was toward the back of the lot.

When my grandfather, John Hise Hastings, and his wife, Edie, traded their farm east of Marion for the State Street property, they made another room by enclosing the side porch, and filled in the cistern. In 1914, when my parents moved there, they put in city water, with a single cold-water faucet in the kitchen.

One of the casualties of the Depression was the running water, which we cut off in 1930. Our next move was to clean out the hard-water well, which had been unused for a number of years.

Two or three young men helped Dad. I remember their taking turns, stripped to the waist, drawing bucket after bucket and pouring the water out on the ground. Rather than lean over the well, they climbed up on the curb, which made the job less tiring, as they could stand erect.

All morning they strained at bucket after bucket, but never did draw the well dry. They finally concluded that most of the brackish water was out. What remained was from an underground stream, clean and fresh enough to drink. We never tested the water, and as far as we knew, no testing facilities were available. Although there was a severe drought throughout the Midwest in the early

thirties, our well never failed to produce an abundance of cold water.

The only problem was the hardness of the water. This we solved by putting a rain barrel at one corner of the house. We saved the soft rain water for shampooing our hair and for the laundry, as far as it would go. In the winter, Mom would sometimes melt snow on the heating stove to get soft water to wash our hair. But it took a lot of snow to make even one gallon of water, so this was not a common practice.

In the summer we took baths in the smokehouse. It had big cracks in the floor where the bath water could be dumped. There were also cracks in the walls, but we presumed no one was looking. In the winter we bathed in the kitchen, where Mom kept a fire in the cookstove until bedtime. No one ever thought of taking a bath in the winter and then going outside.

In the summer we would draw bath water in the morning and set it in the sun until late afternoon. On hot days this was all the heat needed to warm the water. In winter we set tubs of water on the heating stove or the cook stove. Thus we saved any expense for heating water. One or two neighbors had galvanized water heaters in their kitchens, connected to coal ranges, but we never even imagined the luxury of running hot water!

We practiced the same economies with laundry water. In summer we set a wash tub on bricks, about four inches off the ground, and built a fire underneath. In winter the laundry water was heated on the cook stove.

In warm weather Mom set up her laundry bench outdoors and scrubbed the clothes by hand. The bench and tubs were moved indoors in cold weather. The aroma of wet clothes drying indoors on a cold day evokes memories never experienced by those accustomed only to the whirr of an automatic dryer. Too, the added moisture in the air was good for your sinuses!

We didn't waste even the wash water. We carried it bucket by bucket to water our flowers and vegetables. Mom always believed that soapy water was especially good for rosebushes—kept the bugs off, she thought.

Our water was exceptionally cold, and when we wanted a drink, we merely drew a "fresh" bucket and drank at the well, right from the bucket. One summer we planted a gourd vine by the well, and for two or three years after that used gourds for dippers.

We watered the chickens from the well, and Dad was just as concerned that they have fresh, cold water two or three times a day in hot weather as he was that they have warm water in winter. "Bobby, give the chickens a fresh drink before you go back to play," were typical parting words at the dinner table in the summer.

Dad, hot and sweaty from working in the garden, would often draw a full bucket, turn it up to his lips, and then let some of it spill down his neck and shoulders for the cooling effect. Before I was strong enough to lift a whole bucket, I would tip it on the edge of the curb and drink in the same fashion.

Our well also doubled as a refrigerator during the Depression. We bought ice occasionally, but only for tea and lemonade. We put oleo, milk, eggs, and other perishables in a bucket, lowered it within a foot or so of the water level, and tied the rope to a board laid across the curb. Food kept remarkably cool that way. Of course, you couldn't put much food in one bucket, but since we didn't have a whole lot of food to begin with, that was really no problem.

The Walter Lang family, across the street, owned an electric refrigerator, the kind with the coils on top. Melva, their daughter, worked at the Central Illinois Public Service Company, and toward the end of the Depression they traded for a newer model. We felt really lucky when they offered us their old one for practically nothing. Mom made a place for it in the kitchen, and we couldn't wait to get it home.

When the Langs got their new model, they disconnected the old one and let it sit on their back porch for a few days. We were waiting until we could get someone to help us move it—maybe borrow a truck of some kind. But this was poor economy. By the time we moved it, the compressor was "frozen" solid. I can't describe our despair as we looked at that refrigerator, sitting in our kitchen, looking all ready to start making ice cubes, but good for nothing but a storage cabinet.

This story has a happy ending, though, for we priced the repairs and eventually accumulated enough cash to put the refrigerator in working order.

If you were to visit 1404 North State now, you would find the well still there, with its red brick curbing now whitewashed. And although it has stood unused for years, I feel certain the water is as cold and sweet as when I was a boy.

I must admit, however, that I always had just a sliver of boyish superstition when I walked past that well, especially on stormy nights when the wind chased broken clouds across a full moon, for during my boyhood two of our neighbors drowned themselves in their wells.

WIND AND FLOOD AND DUST

Nature was not satisfied to sit on the sidelines during the Great Depression. She had to get in on the act, too.

> When sorrows come, they come not single spies,
> But in battalions . . .   *Hamlet*

Although the hailstorm that hit the north side of Marion in 1930 was purely local, it seemed to typify the rampage of drought, extreme heat and cold, dust, and floods that characterized the thirties.

When I was a boy, it seemed that nearly everyone was afraid of storms except Dad. The stage for fear had been set in Southern Illinois by the most devastating tornado in American history—the storm of March 18, 1925, that slammed through Missouri, Illinois, and Indiana, killing 689 persons. Although it bypassed Marion, it did enough damage in nearby DeSoto and Murphysboro to put the fear of the Lord in anyone's heart.

I often wondered if everyone was as scared of storms as people in Marion. Had the earth always been plagued

by tornadic winds that sucked man and beast screaming
into the air, or by pummeling hailstones that smashed
windows and gouged big holes in housetops?

I think it was the nighttime thunderstorms in March
and April that terrified me most. If it was daytime, we
would study the clouds ("That cloud's yellow—got hail
in it . . . believe it's going to blow over . . . goin' to
be lots of wind in that storm. See how those clouds on
top are boiling up?") Occasionally we might go to a
neighbor's house with a basement, but after the 1930
hailstorm did more damage to the house where we took
shelter than to our own, we took our risks and stayed
home.

Violet Stearns, my cousin, remembers when she and
Ray were married in the early years of the Depression.
They lived in a ramshackle farmhouse in Johnson
County, about a mile from her parents, Marshall and
Alverta Johns. "Mom and Dad had a cellar, and when a
storm came up at night we lit out across the field for
their house. I'll bet I've run a thousand miles from
storms. If we went around by the road, it was farther,
so we always cut across the field."

Violet was not alone. You can't lightly dismiss the
memory of one tornado that kills 689 people.

When a summer cloud was coming up, Dad enjoyed
sitting on the washbench out by the well. If he had been
working in the garden, he would remove his shirt and let
the fresh wind cool him off. He also delighted in watching the movement of storms. In fact, he often stayed outside until the rain had started, delighting in nature's
shower bath. Mom, on the other hand, started closing
windows and locking doors if a cloud grew the least bit
ominous.

She would call for Dad to come inside—three, maybe
four times. Finally, in desperation, "Eldon, me and

Bobby's goin' to the pantry, and I'm lockin' the door.
You can just stay out there and get blowed away for all
I care."

Ours was a five-room frame house, with a windowless
pantry in the middle. In the kitchen was a shelf for the
water bucket and washpan, over which was a towel rack.
A single, unused faucet protruded from the wall over the
water bucket. Also in the kitchen were a green-and-
ivory coal cookstove, an old-fashioned cabinet with a
porcelain countertop and a pullout bin for flour (bought
in 24-pound sacks), and overhead shelves for dishes;
there was a table with six kitchen chairs. On another
shelf was a Seth Thomas eight-day clock Mom and Dad
got as a premium with Larkin Products.

In the dining-sitting room was our heating stove, a
library table where I studied and where the Atwater-
Kent radio sat, and three or four rocking chairs and foot-
stools. Between the dining room and the kitchen was a
two-way china closet, with glass doors opening into both
rooms, where Mom kept her fancy dishes, seldom used.
A colonnade with open shelves separated the dining and
living rooms. In the living room we kept our victrola, an
old-time black leather davinette that made into a bed,
and two horribly outsized matching rockers.

There were two bedrooms, one used only for company
or sickness, and the other closed off, in winter, until
about an hour before bedtime. A single 75-watt bulb
hung from each ceiling by a green electric cord, operated
by a button on the socket for which you groped in the
dark.

In the center was the pantry, where Mom stored
canned fruit, potatoes, quilts and bedding. In summer
we kept our winter clothes in there and in winter, our
summer clothes. It was papered with newspapers, and

I always enjoyed peeling away the layers to read the papers dated five years before, or ten, or maybe even fifteen. It was a lesson in history, layer upon layer. In winter we also kept the chamber pot in there at night, or during the day if someone was ill.

But back to the storms. Evidently Mom thought the pantry was the safest place—or at least the thunder and lightning couldn't be seen or felt as keenly.

In case you are wondering, Dad was never blown away, struck by lightning, or injured by hail, in spite of Mom's predictions. And neither was he ever locked out. When the rain started in earnest, he would make a break for the back door, letting in one big gust of wind and rain before bolting the door securely. Or, if the cloud blew over, he just stayed by the well, later saying, "Now see, as bad as we need rain, you scared it off." It was a common saying that if you discussed a cloud too much it would break up or go around.

Another belief was that a feather pillow or a feather-bed would protect you from lightning. One day my sister, Afton, was struck by lightning while carrying a feather pillow. Ever after, family opinion was divided. "The pillow didn't help a bit," some said. "Yes, it did," others said. "If she hadn't had the pillow, she would have been killed!"

It happened on Sunday, June 19, 1932, in St. Louis. Mom was visiting Afton at the time. A storm blew up, and someone remarked that a feather pillow was good protection. Afton had walked into the bedroom to get a pillow and was just coming back through the doorway when she was struck.

Mom, who for years had been expecting the worst from a storm of some kind, rode with her to the hospital in an emergency police car, and the old *St. Louis Star* had Afton's picture on the front page the next morning! "Stunned in Storm," the cutline read. It went on to describe the "bursts of thunder and flashes of lightning" which shut down *The Riviera Girl* during the third act at the Municipal Opera in Forest Park.

But the little thunderstorms that drove us to pantries or cellars were nothing compared to the record heat and drought of the early thirties, resulting in the dust bowl out West and setting the stage for John Steinbeck's *The Grapes of Wrath*.

Some of the winters in the mid-thirties were unusually severe, particularly that of 1936–37, which brought added misery to Americans already pressed for money to buy fuel and warm clothing.

Most tragic of the natural disasters for our area was the 1937 flood, which struck the Mississippi and Ohio valleys in January, claiming 250 lives. The subfreezing temperatures greatly increased the suffering. I remember this flood vividly, for backwaters from the Ohio River reached into Harrisburg, only twenty miles east of Marion.

My diary for January, 1937, reads, "Rained all day . . . sleeted . . . more rain . . . very cold . . . waters up all along the Ohio, and Shawneetown [Illinois] is completely deserted . . . no immediate danger here in Marion, but lots of refugees here; some moved in the Elks club; our church took up $30 offering for them . . . water up to some chimneys in Harrisburg . . . big fire in Cincinnati . . . Cairo nearly deserted, neighboring schools closed . . . some children separated from parents, with Moms and Dads in one state and kids in another . . . soldier boys [National Guard] standing around town armed.

"Dad went to Harrisburg to help in flood relief . . . Mom went to First Baptist Church to help cook for refugees . . . some refugees may move in with us [never did] . . . expecting Cairo levee to break . . . Red Cross has Tent City out at the fairgrounds; also giving immunizations there . . . rode my bicycle out to fairgrounds to see Tent City . . ."

Residents of Illinois river towns such as Golconda, Cave-in-Rock, Elizabethtown, and Cairo watched as whole houses and barns floated downstream, often with livestock and chickens perched precariously on top. Down the way, these homes would break into ten thousand pieces. Since most insurance policies did not cover flood damage, the loss would be one hundred percent.

On January 20, 1937, classes at school were suspended so we could hear the broadcast of Franklin D. Roosevelt's second inaugural address. Awed by the flood and the other tumultuous events of the thirties, I asked in my diary, "I just wonder who we will hear four years from now and what I will be doing then, even one year from now. And I wonder about our family too . . ."

A DEATH IN APRIL

"Bruno Hauptman is dead."

When these somber words came over our Atwater-Kent radio on Friday night, April 3, 1936, announcing the execution of the kidnapper of Charles Lindbergh, Jr., a hush settled over our family. Yet death seemed far away. After all, it was over nine hundred miles from Marion to the penitentiary at Trenton, New Jersey, where Bruno Hauptman died.

Yet death was nearer than we even faintly imagined. In fact, just five days away. And within twenty-four hours he would announce his coming.

LaVerne, my nearest brother, nine years older than I was, dropped out of high school during the Depression to deliver groceries for Brown and Colombo's store. But the job was short-lived, and he hitchhiked to St. Louis to live with my sister, Afton. He had bad luck catching a ride, and dark caught him halfway, with a rain cloud coming up. He crawled into a haystack near Route 13 for the night, then continued to St. Louis.

My brother-in-law, Frank Wolff, helped him find a job at Nelson Manufacturing Co., which made ice cream cabinets. Work was always better in the spring and summer at Nelson's, and the spring of 1936 found both La-Verne and Frank working even on Saturdays. They lived in a tiny apartment on Madison Street, where they had to cross the back porch to reach the bath they shared with the adjoining apartment.

With two in the family working, they shopped for a better apartment. Then, in a letter postmarked 8:30 P.M. on March 22, 1936, LaVerne wrote that he had "found such a bargain I just couldn't resist it. I got a '28 Oldsmobile for $60. It has five new tires. We will drive home before long. Of course it will take all I make for about two months, but it is worth it."

On Monday morning, March 30, Afton went downtown to pay some bills, and stopped at Stix, Baer & Fuller to write a letter. "We are coming for the weekend. Since Frank and LaVerne work all day Saturday, we will be there about eleven. LaVerne says he is coming especially for a hen dinner . . ."

Saturday morning, April 4, Dad killed the fattest hen in the chicken yard. Mom dressed it, soaked it in salt water a couple of hours, and then set it on the back porch to keep cool until Sunday morning.

When eleven P.M. came, and twelve, and they hadn't yet come, we went to bed. About three A.M. the 1928

Olds pulled up in front of the house. Dad turned on the porch light, the only light in the house operated by a wall switch, and we met them at the door.

"Why LaVerne, you're as white as a sheet," Mom said. "Whatever's wrong, son?"

"Oh, nothing," he replied, trying to minimize her fears. "Just a little upset stomach. Been puking on the way. That's why we're late."

"He went to the doctor after work Friday," Afton filled in. "He has sugar diabetes . . ."

Pneumonia we knew, and tuberculosis (or consumption) and appendicitis and malaria and typhoid and smallpox. But diabetes we didn't.

Reassured that it couldn't be more than a temporary upset, we went to bed. But for some reason, no one could eat much of Mom's baked hen the next day. LaVerne lay around listlessly. By midafternoon it was apparent that he couldn't return to St. Louis.

Monday, April 6, Afton again wrote on Stix, Baer & Fuller notepaper from downtown:

We got home last night at 11:30. It quit raining before we got to Carbondale. The morning Globe says, "Tornado struck five states." The kids slept all the way. How is my sweet brother? Mother, I could eat some of your good dinner now, but yesterday I couldn't have no appetite with the storm, and LaVerne sick.

I sure miss you. I put your old work cap and shirt in the closet. They look just like you. I know you will be better if you stay down there all week and eat good and rest. Your job will be waiting for you and we will take care of the car. I told our landlord we are moving and he said that was perfectly alright if we want to better ourselves. I told him about you. He said as long as you were under 35, you would be completely cured, and for you to go out to the Barnes' Clinic and they had a great specialist and by being on a regular diabetic diet and doctoring it would only be a short time for a cure. . . ."

Back in Marion, LaVerne lay around the house all of Monday, still and pale. Dad and Frank had taken him the day before to our family doctor, W. G. Parmley, who often opened his office on Sunday morning for emergency cases. Dr. Parmley showed no apprehension, feeling that a series of insulin shots would soon put LaVerne back on his feet.

About the middle of Monday morning, LaVerne said he wanted to lie down back of the heating stove, a favorite napping place. So Mom made a pallet and he stretched out. "LaVerne, I wish you could take a bath, son," she said. "But I'm afraid for you to. It's too cool outside." Then she set what we called the "foot tub" on top of the heating stove to warm some water. "But I do want to wash your feet."

It took both Mom and Dad to help him up from the pallet into a rocker back of the stove. Then Mom got down on her knees and washed his feet.

Tuesday morning, April 7, LaVerne roused us about three A.M., nauseated and almost delirious. Dad pulled on his clothes and walked down State Street to East De Young, then to North Market, and to Dr. Parmley's back door. The two of them rode back in Dr. Parmley's car. By now we knew our enemy was real, although we didn't know how to cope with him. Dr. Parmley merely suggested bigger doses of insulin. But with every shot LaVerne grew weaker.

Nothing was said about hospitalization. The nearest hospital was at Herrin, ten miles away, but some people in Marion had a superstious belief that patients "went there to die." There was Holden Hospital at Carbondale, seventeen miles away, but could they do more than administer insulin? We had no car, no telephone. Not that these would have made a difference, but their absence symbolized our isolation, our hesitancy.

About daybreak on Wednesday, April 8, Sena Sinks, a long-time neighbor, came in the front door. Word had spread through the neighborhood that the death vigil had set in. She sat beside the bed in the front bedroom, alternately dipping strips of white cotton rag in a pan of cold water and bathing LaVerne's hot forehead. The April sun rose and streamed in the east window. Again, someone had gone for Dr. Parmley. But at 6:50 A.M., before the doctor arrived, LaVerne died in Dad's arms.

How do I remember it was 6:50? Because Mom got up after a minute or two, walked to the kitchen, and looked at the Seth Thomas clock that Dad wound each night, saying softly, "He died at 6:50."

It may seem strange that a distraught mother, robbed of a child for the first time, and after only four days of illness, should be concerned with time. I used to wonder about that. But, looking back, I understand. It was her way of accepting the unacceptable, of pinpointing in time her darkest hour. Never once did I hear my parents say, "We just can't believe it's true." It was true. And they faced that reality as they had the hailstorm in 1930, the closing of Old West Side, the sour grapefruit, the WPA, and the hundred-and-one other blows of the thirties.

When Dr. Parmley arrived about 7:30, he and Dad stood behind the heating stove for a few minutes. This old family doctor, now near retirement, opened and closed his hands near the fire, as if to warm them. Then he reached into his pocket for a handkerchief to dry his eyes.

We buried LaVerne on Good Friday, April 10.

After the funeral, some of the folks offered to stay the first night with us. "No," said Dad, "we'll make it. We have to face it sometime. We'll be all right." And after Dad's funeral, years later, Mom insisted that she could stay alone the first night. And she did.

A few days later, when Mom was changing the bedding, she felt a strange lump in the pillow on the bed where LaVerne had died. Opening the pillowcase, she found inside a crown of feathers. The feathers were actually formed into the shape of a circular crown. We showed it to neighbors and relatives. Some said the heat from his temperature had fused the feathers into this strange pattern. Others said it was an omen that the deceased was at rest. Mom carefully wrapped the feathery crown in tissue paper and kept it among her keepsakes for many years. I don't know what eventually became of it.

All that summer we took fresh flowers from our yard to his grave—iris and moss roses in May, day lilies and larkspur in June, zinnias and dahlias in July.

Eleven years later I watched another mother cut flowers from her yard for her boy's grave. It was October, 1947, and I was the student pastor of a little neighborhood church in Ardmore, Oklahoma. The first body of a deceased World War II serviceman from Carter County was being returned. His parents were Mr. and Mrs. Claude Bell, retired farmers and members of our congregation.

Their son's body had been cremated in Manchuria, and a military escort brought the ashes on the Santa Fe from Fort Worth to Ardmore. Since this was the first World War II military funeral in the county, the schools closed. A parade formed at the railroad station, with flags and bands, and a service was held in the civic auditorium. The floral tributes were magnificent, including an American flag formed of red, white, and blue blossoms. The high school chorus sang.

Although the burial case did not come with the urn, we went through the formality of a committal. Then Mr. and Mrs. Bell took the ashes home.

A few mornings later the Harvey Funeral Home called to say that the vault had been delivered and that a driver would come for the Bells and for me.

The Bells were large and plain people. He was wearing bib overalls and she a plain cotton housedress. When they came out to the car, he was carrying the ashes and she had a bouquet of marigolds and black-eyed susans from her back yard. There had been a heavy dew the night before, and her shoes were wet. Dew still clung to the flowers, which she carried in a quart Mason jar, holding it between her two big, brown hands on the way to the cemetery.

Just before the committal, Mrs. Bell asked Mr. Harvey if she could look inside. He hesitated. "Go ahead, it's all right," Mr. Bell reassured him.

Slowly, the mortician unscrewed the cover. Both parents leaned over for a look at the two slivers of whitened bone and the handful of grey ashes. A cry of anguish, originating deep in the mother's bosom, drowned in her throat.

Down her face coursed big tears, falling on the marigolds where they blended with the dew. It was then that I thought of roses and larkspur and dahlias in another cemetery, back in Illinois . . .

A STRING OF LIGHTS FOR CHRISTMAS

Christmas at 1404 North State began when Mom reached for the cardboard box marked "Xmas decorations" on the top shelf of the pantry. First to go up were the ropes of paper garlands, green and red, which she stretched across the living and dining rooms. Where the strands crossed in the center of each room, she suspended a big, red paper bell which folded out like an old-fashioned Valentine heart. From the ropes we hung silvery icicles; in the windows we put red paper wreaths.

Tree ornaments, carefully packed away from previous years, were unwrapped. These included some frayed icicles, brittle with age, which seemed to get shorter each year. If the little metal loop on an ornament was broken, cotton string or hairpins held it to the tree.

White divinity candy and fresh fruit salad were two Christmas musts. The divinity, which Mom always made on a clear, cold day so it would not turn sticky, she beat so long and furiously that you could almost imagine sparks jumping from the wire beater as it went clickity-click-click-clickity-click against the sides of the mixing bowl. And the fruit salad must always have three and only three ingredients: California Sunkist oranges, thick slices of fat, solid bananas, and juicy chunks of Dole pineapple. Grapes, peaches, apples, or other fruits were considered "foreign" to real fruit salad. The salad, always stored on the back porch so it would be icy cold, was served with tall, white slices of homemade angel food cake.

There would be other goodies, such as the golden-brown baked chicken and crisp cold celery on which Aunt Bertha Anderson prided herself (hers was the brownest chicken and the crispest celery in Marion). But more sentiment lingers from the moist, white divinity and the cold fruit salad than from anything else.

One explanation for my nostalgia is what happened the Christmas that members of our grade-school band went from house to house playing carols. Our director, George Ashley, suggested that this might be a way to raise money for new uniforms.

Four of us, who played clarinets, were to come to our house. I dreaded to, because Mom and Dad had said they simply didn't have any cash to give. But we set up our music racks and played "Silent Night" and "O Little Town of Bethlehem." Then Mom went over to the see-through china closet between the kitchen and dining-room and brought out the "depression glass" candy plate, with squares of white and brown and pink candies in each of its sections. Seldom had my friends tasted divinity so smooth and rich, and I will always remember how extravagantly they praised it. Although they were unaware of what it meant to me, what they said eased my boyish embarrassment at being treated with candy instead of money.

If we sent or received Christmas cards, I have no memory of it. Cards and stamps were expendable in the thirties—the few cents they cost were preempted for food and coal and clothing. But there were other ways to show your love.

About December 22, Dad would kill one of his fattest yellow hens. The same morning Mom would dress her, then lay her out on dish cloths to dry. Next the hen was wrapped in white cloths, then in waxed paper or leftover bread wrappers. Finally she went into a box, with wrappings made from paper sacks, and tied with odds and ends of string saved from grocery packages.

Shortly after dinner, Dad would set out for the post office to mail the hen, and the home-baked goodies packed with her in the box, to my sister Afton and her family in St. Louis. We speculated on whether postal regulations permitted uncooked food to be mailed, but we never asked at the window. And the yellow hen was wrapped so securely that no telltale moisture ever leaked through.

So, rather than gifts of clothing or toys, a little chicken that had scratched in the spring grass in a quiet little Southern Illinois town found its way to the table of my sister in the city. We sent what we could, and I always sensed that the package was tied by cords of love.

Afton often sent us a five-pound box of chocolates for Christmas. There was a special big-city glamor to the chocolate-covered cherries, mints, nougats, caramels, and fudges. We would tuck the box away in the front bedroom, which was closed off in the winter. Here the candy kept cold and firm. Once or twice a day we visited the "big icebox" for a treat, choosing first the pieces wrapped in shiny red or gold. Five pounds of candy lasted way up into January, and we savored every day that Christmas was stretched into the new year.

The one luxury I coveted, Christmas after Christmas, was electric lights for our tree. I often dreamed how wonderful it would be if soft, colored lights could glow among the tattered ornaments we had preserved from the more prosperous twenties.

If I ever want to feel a lump in my throat some dark December day, I relive an afternoon when Mom took me to the Christmas party of her Ladies' Aid, in the home of Mrs. Frank Miles at 1208 North Glendale. Although forty Christmases have come and gone, I can still retrace our steps as we entered a sort of side room or sun porch with several windows, where Mrs. Miles had decorated a fir tree with real electric lights. I recall the sheer ecstasy of lying on the floor, gazing in awe at the lights, so close you could touch them, so near you could feel their tiny warmth.

A big Christmas tree with real lights always stood in the main auditorium of the First Baptist Church. And although James Sneddon, the custodian with the Scottish accent, was never known for being stingy when it came to firing the church furnace, there was an emotional warmth that exceeded the eighty degrees on the thermometer. It was the glow of those red, green, and blue Christmas lights.

Many churches no longer erect Christmas trees in their sanctuaries, fearing they are out of harmony with the true meaning of the holiday. But I will always be grateful that someone in my boyhood church took the time to trim and light a big tree whose beauty I could absorb for two or three Sundays each December.

As I walked to church on December evenings, or to a neighbor's, or to town, I picked my route along streets where I could see the most lights. As soon as I passed one house with a lighted tree, I looked for the next one. The windows with Christmas lights formed a bridge for my imagination, a light-strewn path that led me right on to Christmas.

Somehow, one year, I discovered a 60-watt red light bulb in the house. It gave me an idea. Why not screw the bulb into the overhead socket that hung from the ceiling? It would cast a red glow on the tree, and the reflection on the icicles might look like an actual string of lights. We tried it. Turning out the other lights, Mom, Dad, and I went outside and stood in the winter darkness, right in front of the window where we could see the tree bathed in the soft, red glow of the single overhead bulb.

"Look, it's just like real," I cried excitedly. And for a few moments of imagination we did have a string of real lights.

Lum and Abner, the popular radio show of the thirties, repeated the same Christmas skit each year. A young couple on their way to the county seat to pay year-end taxes got as far as Pine Ridge, Arkansas, locale of Lum and Abner's Jot-'Em-Down Store. Here, stopped by a snowstorm, they sought shelter in a nearby barn. The good folks of Pine Ridge, who discovered that the young woman was pregnant, quickly came to their rescue. They arranged for food, blankets, and heat, and then sent for a doctor. On that cold, star-filled night a baby was born.

In the closing episode, Lum and Abner were walking through the snow, carrying a box of home-cooked victuals to the barn. They waxed philosophical as Lum said, "You know, Abner, here we are, two old codgers, our lives about over, and here's this young-un', just comin' into the world . . . sort of like that first Christmas, years and years ago. . . ."

As Dad reached over to turn off the Atwater-Kent, he said, "You know, if that wouldn't give a fellow the Christmas spirit, I don't know what could."

No one else said anything. But deep inside, the three of us felt real good, real warm, real Christmasy. And suddenly the lights were shining all over our end of town!

AUNT BERTHA AND UNCLE CHARLEY

J. M. Gordon and Sarah Bradley Gordon reared five children in Johnson County, a poor yet pastoral setting. Including its little county seat of Vienna (population 1,094, the highest in the county), it also embraces such metropolises as Buncombe, Goreville, Tunnel Hill, Cypress, and Ozark.

Grandpa Gordon, who came from Georgia, and other early settlers, many from Kentucky and Tennessee, evidently liked the rolling hills of Johnson County because it reminded them of Appalachia, though they could barely squeeze a living out of the clay soil.

Visit certain sections of Tennessee, Kentucky, and North Carolina, and to this day you will find similarities in speech, attitudes, food, and religion between their residents and the people of Johnson County.

Grandpa and Grandma Gordon had one son, Pleas, a country schoolteacher who died in 1901 at the age of 26. They had four daughters—Bertha, Alverta, Mattie, and Ruby, my mother. These four sisters and their husbands were very compatible. Each girl was an excellent cook, loved good food, and liked to entertain company. At one time the four sisters easily had a combined weight of nearly a thousand pounds!

Two lived in Marion—Aunt Bertha and Uncle Charley
Anderson and my parents, Ruby and Eldon Hastings.
Two lived on farms in Johnson County—Aunt Alverta
and Uncle Marshall Johns and Aunt Mattie and Uncle
Bob Wollaver.

During the Depression, when there was little else to do,
these four families spent many days entertaining and
cooking for each other. Nor did they wait for an invitation or send notice of a visit. They visited as often as
they could and with as little formality as possible.

Aunt Bertha was the dearest to me, perhaps because
she lived nearest and I was there so often. I passed her
house at 108 West White, just a block from the Illinois
Central station, on my way to town, to the movies, to
church, and to school.

The six-room house included both a living room and a
parlor, as well as a dining-sitting room. In the winter, she
and Uncle Charley sealed themselves in the dining-sitting
room, where they hugged the open fire. Some nights they
might never turn on a light except to go to bed. The
grate spilled ashes and soot and smoke all over, but they
liked it. When I was a small boy wanting to tend the
fireplace, she had me believing that poking the fire would
make me wet the bed.

Only when company came did they open up the living
room and build a fire in their big, square, red Heatolator.
And never—not even once—did I see anyone sit in their
parlor, which was complete with mohair furniture covered with hand-crocheted doilies, a floor lamp with a
fringe of glass droplets, and a big wicker rocker with
deep side pockets for magazines.

Occasionally I tiptoed in there when no one was looking and sat in one of the big chairs. Oh yes! She did use
that parlor once in 1928 when she entertained a women's
circle from the First Methodist Church.

In the kitchen was a big black cookstove that burned wood or coal, plus an attached galvanized water heater that hissed and shook if it got too hot. At the end of the house, like an afterthought, was an indoor bathroom, so far from her little fireplace that Bertha's chief worry in winter was that the plumbing would freeze.

A quick, energetic woman, she prided herself on how speedily she cooked breakfast. She would lay the paper and kindling in the stove the night before. When the big clock on the courthouse struck six, she would hurry to the kitchen, slosh a generous dose of kerosene on the kindling, strike a match, and the fire would roar away as if the stove itself were going right up the chimney.

With a few brisk movements she slid a pan of biscuits into the oven, and in minutes breakfast was ready. And when she called, you had better come. She didn't like a warmed-over biscuit or cold gravy.

Tramps often stopped at 108 West White during the Depression, since the Andersons lived just a couple of blocks from the "Hoover Hotel," the Illinois Central water tanks where hoboes camped on winter nights. Some said Aunt Bertha's house was marked. But she never turned anyone away, and often prepared a hot dish of fresh food if there were no leftovers. Aunt Bertha didn't believe in leftovers, anyway.

She had three extravagances—at least, that's what my Mom thought they were.

She baked hot bread twice a day, and usually two or three times as much as she and Uncle Charley could eat. But she never served it the second day. "I like good bread, and I want plenty of it. If I want to throw some away, that's my business."

She loved crisp crackers. She bought them in a tiny quarter-pound box. Since we never bought crackers in under the two-pound size, Mom would fuss at her,

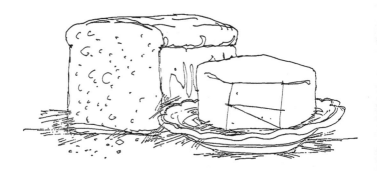

"Bertha, do you realize what you're paying for those little boxes?" And Bertha countered, "I don't care. When I eat a cracker, I want a fresh one, or I'd just as soon do without."

Her third extravagance was creamery butter. Had she not served real butter, I would hardly have known the taste of anything other than oleomargarine during the Depression. She frequently said, "Oleo isn't fit for a hog to eat!" She could also bake the brownest hen, her lemon meringue pie never failed, and she always found the crispest celery in town for Thanksgiving dinner.

Her first husband, Marshall Jack, had died in a mine accident. Uncle Charley, her second husband, was also a miner, a big man with bushy white hair and fat jowls that hung limp on his shirt collar. Like other miners, he had more idle days than work days during the Depression.

He was an ardent Republican. He blamed the Democrats for the Depression and every other ill that befell man or beast, whether it was the '37 flood or the Dust Bowl of '33. In fact, I was grown before I realized that possibly not *all* Democrats wore horns. Even today, if I vote for a Democratic candidate I look around guiltily to see if Uncle Charley is watching.

His bible was the *St. Louis Globe–Democrat*, a staunchly Republican paper. He not only read each morning's paper—he digested it and then regurgitated it all day to whomever would listen. He majored in the editorial page and the political columnists.

He had a good memory, and could quote exactly how many little pigs President Roosevelt had drowned in the Mississippi River, how many acres of wheat he had plowed under, and how many extra Supreme Court justices he wanted on the bench (around a thousand, to hear him tell it).

He could also spiel off statistics on the gross national product, the unemployment rate, the stock market, and the size of the relief rolls.

As a boy, I sat around the grate or, in the summer, on their front porch, and listened in awe to his diagnosis of the economy. And I thought, "Oh, if someone in Washington just realized how much my Uncle Charley knows, and would listen, we could lick this Depression." But no one did.

Aunt Bertha's daughter by her first marriage, Lela Jack, went to St. Louis to work and married a Catholic, Frank Bock, who was also a Democrat. Not a radical, by any means. In fact, very non-verbal. But to Uncle Charley even the label you wore was radicalism.

So whenever Frank and Lela planned a visit, Bertha gave Uncle Charley his "marching orders." She would start a week ahead. "Now Charley Anderson, I want you to listen to me." Using his full name, in contrast to the affectionate "Darb" of everyday conversation—"Now, Charley Anderson, Frank and Lela are coming. They'll only be here a couple of days. And while they are, I want you to forget the *Globe*. I want you to forget the Republican Party. I don't want to hear Roosevelt's name even mentioned. Nor the Supreme Court, the little pigs, the

NRA or the WPA, the Stock Market or the New Deal. If you can't think of anything decent to talk about, just keep quiet."

And that's about what he did. Like an obedient boy getting ready for Christmas, he never used the bad words.

But as soon as Frank and Lela walked down to the IC to catch the train back to Carbondale, and then St. Louis . . .

AUNT ALVERTA AND UNCLE MARSHALL

Alverta and Marshall Johns somehow raised six children on one of the scrubbiest pieces of land in Johnson County. Although I never understood how Marshall could grow anything on such wornout land, he often had enough vegetables, fresh meat, and sorghum molasses to peddle in Marion. Sometimes he sold from his wagon at the hitchrack about a block northeast of the public square. Other times he would peddle from door to door.

He grew his own sorghum cane, which he ground into molasses with a one-horse mill. When his children were all home, he kept back fifty gallons for "table use." It was sorghum on hot biscuits for breakfast, sorghum on hot cornbread for dinner, sorghum on cold cornbread for supper, and more sorghum on cold cornbread at bedtime if, say, they had walked over to Bethlehem Church for night services.

Dad often said that "Marshall Johns is the finest man that ever lived." We enjoyed visiting the Johns, whose farm was twelve miles south of Marion, as often as we could get a ride with someone. Occasionally we rode the

C&EI train to Goreville, where they would meet us in a wagon or car.

Their unpainted farmhouse stood precariously on sandstones piled at each corner, and the winter wind blew unchallenged through a big crack under their front door. With chickens and dogs roaming freely over the yard and under the house, there was little need for a lawn mower. They swept the yard with a broom, and Aunt Alverta hefted the dishwater out the back door.

If we surprised Aunt Alverta and Uncle Marshall, it seemed to please them more than if they had known our plans for a month. Whether we came by wagon or car, we usually walked up the short but extremely steep hill that led to their house. This last stretch of dirt road was more like a rock-bottomed creek bed, and the slightest rain made the rocks slippery as ice.

Aunt Alverta, barefoot in summer, would run out of the house, apron tail flying, to stand in the yard by the time we reached the top of the hill.

"Where in the world do you think you're going? You've caught me in the awfullest mess anybody ever seen. Not a thing on the place to eat, not a bite. How is my sweet sister? And Eldon, you sweet thing. I've never been so glad to see anyone in my life. Come in the house, if you can get in . . . Marshall, kick that lazy hound off the steps . . ."

Once we were inside, with our coats and scarves and gloves off, she went into action like a mess sergeant. "Cecil Ray, go chop some stove wood, and get some big pieces, too. I want a hot fire. And Cora Belle, run to the cellar and grab a pan of 'taters and a couple jars of beans and peaches. Marshall, go kill a hen right quick—no, kill that hateful old rooster . . ."

Each of the four sisters had a specialty. Aunt Bertha excelled in baked chicken, hot biscuits, and lemon pie.

Aunt Mattie had a way with fried country ham and multi-layered banana cakes smothered with butterscotch frosting. Mom was known for her coleslaw, dumplings, banana pudding, and angel food cake.

Aunt Alverta took the honors with her strawberry shortcake. Mom said it was because she was so extravagant with the lard and sugar. Strawberry shortcake a la Johnson County wasn't made with sponge cake or biscuit dough. Instead, Alverta rolled pie crust in flat sheets, baked it, and then broke it in uneven pieces into the sugared strawberries, which she had crushed with her hands. She made shortcakes in a big, deep crock, putting a layer of crust, a layer of strawberries. She soaked her shortcake about three hours—Mom preferred about a one-hour soak.

Regardless, it was heavenly!

Uncle Marshall, a short, godly man, always had a "youngun" on his lap when he ate. He liked children of all ages, and his patience was inexhaustible. Dad came on him unexpectedly one day, kneeling in an open field and praying for rain.

During the Depression, when Dad grew despondent over having nothing to do, he would "strike out for the country for a few days," making Uncle Marshall's his headquarters. He always felt welcome to stay as long as he wished. If there was no other way, he would hitch a ride to Goreville and walk out to their farm. In season, he would get in a little rabbit or squirrel hunting, or help Uncle Marshall or Uncle Bob with the planting or harvesting. He always came home buoyed up.

Aunt Alverta had a number of unusual expressions. "Ain't this the coldest weather that anyone ever did hear tell of *in their lives?*" "Ain't these the hottest times that anyone ever did hear tell of *in their lives?*" "Ain't that the smartest baby that anyone ever did see *in their lives*?"

She had a way of taking a nickel tablet and writing letters that exuded old-fashioned warmth and friendliness. On May 17, 1910, she wrote to Mom from Creal Springs:

Hello Sis, how are you and have you taken the smallpox yet? Why didn't you and Eldon come Sunday? Was lots of people there. Mattie and Ezra [Casey] is going to stay and go to Webbtown [Church] Sunday. Ruby, I am like you. I hate my hat. Do you go to Ma's and Bertha's often? I would like to see you all. You and Eldon come down again.

So . . . no more, answer soon. Alverta.

Another letter, near the end of the Depression, shows the same spirit.

Hello my dear sweet sister and all the rest. How are you feeling this morning? I sure hope you are better. This leaves us OK. The rheumatism hurt Marshall awful bad last night. Wasn't yesterday an awful dark, lonely day? Charlie and Gardner took dinner with us. Where did you spend yesterday? Guess you didn't look for us Sunday. It was awful bad. Now don't never look for us when its snowing and raining, for that Saturday really give me a scare. Well, guess Charley hasn't got back on his job. It's a shame. Sure hope he gets something. Marshall needs a job so bad this pretty weather, but will never get nothing.

Well, I guess you heard the news before now that Mr. and Mrs. Lowery are separated. Mag and Daphine moved away last Friday. I hate it awful bad. She will be missed more than anyone ever moved out of this county. It grieves me and Mar-

shall awful bad . . . All poor old Bethlehem
[Church] likes [lacks of] being dead is just shutting
the doors. So no more about that . . . Now you
have all got a chance to come and I can't go to save
my life, only as I can get someone to stay with Ma.
So come just when you take a notion. Now I started
this letter yesterday but the mail man comes on so
early that I didn't get it done. So I will go mail it
now. Close with lots of love, your sis, Alverta.

A poignant letter written on January 19, 1942, describes
their son, Cecil, just before he left for overseas:

You know Cecil wrote us that he wanted to call us
over long distance telephone Saturday night, said he
wanted to hear his Dad's, mine, and Cora's voice
once again, but said he would let us know later. So
we didn't hear any more, and Marshall just would go
[to a telephone] for fear he had wrote and we hadn't
got the letter. So we did and stayed until 11 o'clock
and no call. So got a letter today and Cecil said there
wasn't any telephone he could get to. He was nearly
killed about it. He is still in California. It troubles
us so bad we can't hardly live. The worst war in this
world. Gets worse all the time. It will kill everybody
before it is over. Cecil sent his pretty cap to me that
he wore when he was at home. I cry every time I
look at it. He said he couldn't wear it no more. Poor
fellow, I don't know what he wears now unless it is a
steel hat . . .

Her letter was prophetic. They never heard his voice
again. Cecil Ray died in the invasion of Okinawa on
May 3, 1945.

A reader who did not know Aunt Alverta might think
she was given to despondency. It was not that, but
rather her ability to express her emotions freely, both

orally and on paper. Perhaps because of this, she actually wore the world like a loose garment, and family and friends gravitated to her door. She was unashamedly human.

AUNT MATTIE AND UNCLE BOB

Aunt Mattie, the second oldest of my mother's sisters, had been married to Ezra Casey and John Albright. John died in a mine accident, and Ezra left home October 18, 1911, on the eight A.M. train from Marion to Carbondale, never to return. Mattie thought he was headed for work at the Carterville District Mine. Just before Christmas he wrote a letter, enclosing $50 for the house payments and gifts and asking her not to try to find him. She did try, but she failed.

From the time I remember, she was married to Bob Wollaver. When I asked which of her three husbands she loved best, she grinned sheepishly, "I loved them all just about the same."

Aunt Mattie and Uncle Bob also lived on a Johnson County farm, just across the road from the Bethlehem Baptist Church, about a mile west of Aunt Alverta and Uncle Marshall.

Like her three sisters, Aunt Mattie enjoyed cooking, and loved to eat. She would work as hard as anyone to set a fine table. But after dinner she went to bed without apology. "Now we're not going to wash a dish. Just let them set. That'll give me something to do when you go home."

"They'll be harder to wash after they set," Mom would say.

"Don't care. When my younguns was little, I had a sick spell, and my doctor said if I went right to bed after dinner, I would never take the TB."

When visiting us, or anyone, she did the same. "You don't wash my dishes, and I'm not going to wash yours," she would laugh as she headed for the bedroom, where she was soon asleep. Her formula apparently worked, for she never "took the TB." As I write this she is eighty-four, strong for her age, and still taking a nap every afternoon.

One night we were sitting at their supper table when Uncle Bob pushed his chair back and said, "I just wish Herbert Hoover and his wife would set down to a meal at our house. If he could see how poor folks eat, there'd be some changes up there in Washington."

Although he spoke in jest, I fully expected, as a small boy with a big imagination, to see a limousine pull up in front of their house some day, out of which the President would emerge and say, "Bob, we've come for dinner!"

A favorite expression on my mother's side of the family was, "Now we're just poor folks. Don't have a lot of style. If you don't see what you want, just ask for it, and if we've got it, you can have it. Just reach and help yourselves."

What that really meant was, "We're tickled to death to have you eat with us, and anything in the house is yours for the asking. Don't worry about manners. Just eat and enjoy yourselves as if this were your home."

Uncle Bob was an energetic farmer who couldn't wait to do his work. In the summer he would often hitch his team in the dark and be standing at the edge of the cornfield with his plow when the first streaks of dawn gave enough light to see the rows.

Uncle Bob was also an ardent Democrat—as strong as Uncle Charley Anderson was a Republican. Bob blamed the Depression on the Republicans, and Charley blamed

it on the Democrats. There was no middle ground. Uncle
Bob took no newspapers and paid little attention to the
radio. Uncle Charley was always loaded with statistics
and quotations. Uncle Bob was no match for him; he
knew where he stood, but not exactly why.

So when we got together the sparks flew, and you wondered where they might stop. But one of them always
backed down, after an inevitable climax.

Exhausted of patience, and backed into a corner by
Charley's arguments, Uncle Bob would shift his chewing
tobacco from one cheek to the other, get up from his
rocking chair, and go over and spit in the coal bucket.
Then, his neck and face reddening, and with quivering
voice, he would say, "Dammit to hell, Charley Anderson,
I don't care if I was a-starvin' to death, I wouldn't vote
for no Republican."

And that was that. The room got deathly still. In a
few minutes the drift of conversation turned to the crops,
the weather, or when the old sow would farrow, while the
burden of government shifted back to Washington.

The third Sunday of May was decoration day and
homecoming at Bethlehem Church and cemetery across
the road from the Wollavers. This annual event held a
lot of sentiment for our family, since I was born on a
Saturday night before a third Sunday in May. That Sunday, in 1924, Dad drove down to Bethlehem in his Model
T to deliver the birth announcement in person.

It was a typical country homecoming, with a memorial
service in the morning, dinner on the ground, and singing
in the afternoon. We often made a weekend of it, going
down on Saturday.

Old Bethlehem school once stood near the church, and
Aunt Mattie remembers going one term, about 1895,
when her brother, Pleas, was the teacher. "Pleas asked
me to spell 'are,' " she recalls, "and I wouldn't do it, just
for meanness, so he whupped me."

At the annual homecoming, my great uncle, Charlie Bradley, raised money to keep the cemetery cleaned off for another year. Over the years he developed quite a reputation as a fund raiser.

A short, red-headed fellow with deep-set, pale blue eyes, he made his first plea in the morning service, usually without fanfare. During the noon hour he circulated among the menfolk who had stood outside during church, and hit them for a donation. If he didn't have enough by the two o'clock service—say $6, which would pay someone $1 a month from April to September—he really put on the arousements.

"Now folks," he led off in his country whang, "I want you to listen to me real good. How would you like to come here next year and see all these graves grown up in weeds, so you couldn't even read the tombstones? It's a shame and a disgrace to this community, how little money I've raised today. Don't ask me how much—I'm ashamed to say. But this is the last time I'm agonna ask you. I've done my part, and my conscience is clear. So it's up to you now, if that's the kind of people you want to be."

He always got his $6.

THE OVERALL CLASS

How would you describe a third grade teacher who made every boy in school wish he had no Sunday pants —only overalls?

Edith Norman Greathouse did that at the Jefferson School in Marion, the years she also taught a boys' class at the First Methodist Church.

Only this was no ordinary Sunday School class. First, it met in a house next door to the big Methodist Church on West Main Street. Second, you had to wear overalls. If you could afford dress pants, you went to regular classes.

Mrs. Norman built this class up so that I regretted owning a Sunday pair of pants and a slipover sweater. She enrolled a big class of boys from all over town who otherwise might not have attended because they didn't have the clothes. And her descriptions of their watermelon feeds and ice cream socials didn't hurt the attendance, either.

She did her recruiting on public school time. But since it was a long way from Marion to Washington, D.C., the Supreme Court never questioned her.

Mrs. Norman was a fun-loving woman who enjoyed telling stories, playing the piano, and explaining the sharps and flats so simply that anyone could understand. At one time she had played the organ at the old silent movies, improvising the melodies as she went along, to match the plot. If she ever needed a sheet of music to play anything, we never knew it.

After lunch each day, about twenty-five minutes were set aside for story time. These stories were unique—she made them up as she went along. They were continued from day to day, and a story might require as much as six weeks to tell.

This was a sure cure for absenteeism, because everyone waited breathlessly for the next installment. One story I remember told of two lads playing in a dry river bed out west when a flash flood cut them off from the shore. I must have missed a day—I can't for the life of me remember how they ever got home.

Another story, a true one, helped me more than she could possibly have realized. She recalled her experiences as a rural schoolteacher—how the children brought jugs of milk and set them in the moist dirt under the schoolhouse to keep cool. She described their lunches of big homemade biscuits and country ham. "How I envied those biscuits and ham," she smiled, "when I pulled out my little store-bought bologna and crackers."

The point was, I sometimes took biscuit sandwiches in my lunch—usually bacon or egg. I didn't want to take biscuits. I wanted store-bought "light bread." When we had no store bread, Mom made my sandwiches with biscuits. I felt a stigma from the biscuits, and after taking a bite I would drop my hand inside the lunch sack to hide what I was holding.

But after Mrs. Norman glorified those country biscuits, I never felt the same about them again. Somehow the stigma was gone, and they looked and tasted as good as light bread.

OSHKOSH B'GOSH

A group picture made in 1932 of the second grade at the old Jefferson School in Marion shows twenty-three of the thirty boys wearing the standard Depression uniform—bib overalls and a cotton shirt. Six had on long pants and, heaven forbid, one was wearing short pants with long white stockings!

The arrival of the Sears catalog each August signaled the time to buy school clothes. Each fall the same order was mailed to Chicago. Two pairs of bib overalls. Two cotton shirts. Two pairs of long-handled underwear. And two pairs of long brown stockings, which would be held in place with a safety pin to your underwear. Shoes we would buy in Marion to make sure of a fit.

The few clothes I had fell into three categories—school clothes, play clothes, and Sunday clothes.

School clothes consisted of the new overalls and blue cotton shirts. Play clothes were last year's school clothes, with the overall legs cut off for summer. Sunday clothes were a pair of wool or corduroy pants, a white shirt, and a long-sleeved slipover sweater. In summer, Sunday clothes would be cotton pants and a sport shirt. When I entered first grade in 1930, I boasted a pair of Sunday tweed knickers with elastic gathered at the knees and knee-length argyle socks. Happily, I soon graduated to long pants.

The very first order of business after school was to change into play clothes. One reason was to cut down on laundry, which was done by hand. The other was to make the good overalls last as long as possible.

Although few and simple, my clothes were adequate and clean, even if I did wear the same pair of overalls for a week, and changed underwear only on Saturday nights. In a quart jar Mom saved every button that ever came off an old shirt or dress. Every size, color, and shape imaginable was in that jar. She also kept a ready supply of patches—the tail of an old shirt to mend the sleeve of a new shirt, and last winter's overalls to patch a busted knee in this year's. Pumping its old-fashioned foot treadle, she knew how to make her 1910 Singer sewing machine hum. Taking as her motto "A stitch in time saves nine," she never let a rip or tear get a head start on her nimble fingers. On our meager cash income, I always had something presentable to wear, not because we could afford an abundance, but because we took care of what we had.

As an example of making clothes last, let me tell you about a winter coat I wore all through grade school. It also doubled as a raincoat for those eight years.

If this sounds like a tall story, you didn't know my Mom. When she bought clothes for a boy, she believed in getting them big enough. She didn't look at the size today, but how the same shirt or coat would look on a growing boy two or three years hence.

So that first coat, with a black rubber-like finish and yellow sheepskin lining, plus a big collar with the same downy lining, wasn't chosen for a six year old. It was bought to last! In all fairness, Mom didn't expect it to last eight winters. It was the Depression that lasted!

Each September I would take it down from the nail where it had hung in the pantry all summer, and try it on. And for seven Septembers Mom would say, "Bobby, I believe to my soul you can get another year's wear out of that coat!"

As I said, it hadn't been made for a six year old. The first day I wore it to school it reached almost to my ankles. My arms were completely swallowed up. I didn't need gloves. I must have looked like a midget wearing a man's overcoat. By the eighth grade it was more like a jacket, with the sleeves almost to my elbows.

But it was warm, and I developed a sentimental attachment to my "sheepskin." Except on rainy days, when the sentiment vanished along with the sunshine. The slick fabric absorbed none of the rain, so the water ran down my pantlegs. And as I grew taller the water line climbed higher.

Snow was even worse, for as it melted, the water that ran down my trousers was icy cold. Somewhere along the years, when the water line was about midway between my waist and my knees, I asked myself "I wonder if they make boys' coats that keep you dry?" I really did, and I really meant it.

Matching the coat was a black, leather-like helmet, also with yellow sheepskin lining. It was an aviator-type cap, with flaps that covered both ears and buckled under your chin. Most exciting were the celluloid goggles that snapped in place to "protect" your eyes from driving rain and sleet.

The helmet was relatively short-lived, maybe to the third grade. Mom wanted me dressed warmly during

those Illinois winters, but at least she didn't try to strangle me.

But back to those bib overalls. They were the thing. Two deep slash pockets in front. Two hip pockets. And pockets across the front for pencils, combs, and what have you. The two adjustable suspender straps hooked over metal buttons in front. If the overalls were too long, you either rolled up the legs or drew up the straps. After they had been washed a few times and had shrunk, you could wear them without rolling a cuff or shortening the straps. But woe if your mother believed in buying overalls "plenty long," for you might choke yourself by pulling the straps too taut!

When I was in fifth grade Mom came home from Powell's "Best Clothes in Egypt" with a genuine pair of Oshkosh B'Gosh overalls. What mid-Depression luxury, I'll tell you! I never went back to another pair of Sears'.

You see, Oshkosh had four snaps on each side. If they fit well, the snaps would hold the side flaps snug up under your armpits. Only the high-school boys didn't button all four snaps. They allowed the two top ones to flap loose. What a mark of masculinity and maturity. Overalls that flapped loose on the sides!

"Now Bobby, keep those overalls fastened up the side. They'll keep out a lot of cold wind, and they look neater, anyway." So I always made sure all four buttons were snapped just before I got home from school.

Underwear also carried a status of sorts, methodically organized into three subdivisions. There was winter underwear, summer underwear, and underwear for spring and fall. Winter underwear was the long unions, tucked in at the ankles under your socks, buttoned down the front, and with a drop seat. Spring and fall underwear was long underwear with the sleeves and legs cut off. Summer underwear was the old-style one-piece BVD's, made of nainsook, that hung like a sack. I really felt grown up when I wore my first two-piece summer underwear, with separate shorts and sleeveless undershirts.

I couldn't help but feel self-conscious about long underwear. For some reason I got it into my mind that long underwear was for country boys. And although we lived just the second house inside the city limits, I very much wanted to be known as a city boy, even if Marion boasted a population something less than ten thousand. So at school I was careful that my underwear didn't show below my shirt cuffs.

I also determined that when I started to high school, there would be no more long unions. I knew we would undress for gym. And I could imagine no greater humiliation than to strip down to long johns while other boys were going around in their shorts, even in the coldest months.

So in my diary of March 20, 1938, is an historic entry. "Changed into shorter underwear today." That was the last day I ever wore long underwear to school. Mom capitulated to the changing times. When I entered high school that fall, I was allowed to wear a briefer style "even if you do catch your death of cold."

There is also significance in the word "shorter" on March 20. "Shorter" underwear meant long unions cut down. "Short" underwear was too daring until nearer May 1.

"DON'T TAKE OFF YOUR UNDERWEAR . . ."

I had very few rules laid down for me in my boyhood, but four "don'ts" stick in my memory. Maybe because I heard them so often. They dealt with self-preservation, health, and food, all of which were pretty basic if you expected to weather the Depression. For each of the four "don'ts" Mom cited a precedent. It was almost like quoting Scripture.

1. "Don't take off your winter underwear until the weather turns warm." The precedent here was my second cousin, Charles Rodd, a high-school student. He stayed after school one night to play basketball. He made the horrible mistake of taking off his winter underwear in the gym and not putting it back on to walk home through a driving rain. Charles came down with a terrific cold and sore throat. From then on, taking off your winter underwear was known to lead not only to colds and sore throats, but also to sinus, fever, chills, bronchitis, tonsillitis, strep throat, headaches, infected mastoids, flu, pneumonia, tuberculosis, chest pains, ear abscess, chest soreness, swelling of the lymph glands, and whooping cough.

2. "Don't eat green grapes." Not that I ever wanted to, but my oldest brother, Gordon, did—to his regret. "Now wait until those grapes turn a good purple," Mom would remind me each summer. "Remember that when Gordon ate them green he had convulsions and climbed the bed posts. We thought he would die." Every summer when I saw grapes hanging green on the vines, I also saw my brother writhing in pain and climbing the bed posts. It wasn't hard to wait until the grapes ripened.

3. "Don't go swimming in those mine pits. If you step off in one of those holes we never would find you. And besides, that mine water has sulphur in it." There were many abandoned strip mines, some only a mile or so out the Spillertown road, and many of the deep cuts were filled with polluted water. Lots of boys slipped off to

swim in them, but although Mom could cite no precedent of a local drowning, her description of the bottomless pits of green, sulphurous water was sufficient. I compromised by swimming in the public pool at nearby Johnston City.

4. "Don't drop the bucket in the well." During the Depression we used the well as our refrigerator, placing eggs, butter, and milk in a bucket and lowering it to just above the water level. Food kept remarkably cool there. But there was always the possibility of tipping the contents. So when I lowered or raised the bucket Mom's precedent was cousin Cecil Ray Johns. "Now remember when Cecil Ray was drawing a jug of buttermilk out of their well and let it break against the side? That milk soured the whole well, and you remember they had to haul drinking water for two or three days, until they could get it cleaned out." So I remembered Cecil Ray and his broken jug of buttermilk, and I retrieved ours safely every time!

A SKELETON IN THE BERRY PATCH

As midsummer approached, we began inquiring where the best blackberries were. Then, up before sunrise, armed with buckets and pans, splashed with kerosene to keep off the chiggers, and wearing long-sleeved shirts against the briars, we started "berry-pickin'." This was not a summertime diversion but an economic necessity, for berries meant jelly and cobblers and pies, and they were free to those with the initiative to find and gather them.

I never cared for berry-pickin' time. I wasn't glad to see it come, and I wasn't sorry to see it go. Especially after some berry-pickers found a skeleton under a tree out by the Henderson-Wallace mine. The man had been missing for days and, as I remember, died from a self-inflicted gunshot wound.

The Depression pushed the suicide rate from 13.6 deaths per 100,000 population in 1928 to a high of 17.4 per 100,000 in 1932. When a neighbor of Uncle Charley Anderson's shot himself to death on a bright, sunny morning in 1938, I wrote in my diary, "I guess it was money matters." Whether that was true I don't know, but that's what the neighbors said.

Looking back, it does seem that an unusual number of people around Marion took their own lives in the space of these few bitter years. One night a man who lived in one of the big brick houses near the center of town bludgeoned his wife and four children to death, so it was said, with a furnace shaker and then jumped into the well in his yard. My brother Gordon, who at the time was delivering for the Marion City Dairy, left milk at their back porch early the next morning, before the bodies were discovered.

Whether the problem was money or a disappointment in love I'm not sure, but another neighbor of ours leaped to her death in the family well. Years later her mother became depressed after the death of her husband and worried about money. One day she went home, gave her house a good cleaning, did some redecorating, burned all the family mementoes and pictures, and then jumped into the same well her daughter had drowned in.

When I was in third grade, one of my favorite teachers went home from school one afternoon to find her husband dead from asphyxiation. Closing the windows and doors, and stuffing the cracks, he had turned on the kitchen gas range. The day before she returned to school, our principal called us together. "Now your teacher has been through a great tragedy. When she comes back tomorrow, please don't mention what happened."

Perhaps that was characteristic of the Great Depression and its victims. You just didn't talk about it unless you had to.

HIRSCHVOGEL

Fall began the afternoon I came home from school and sniffed the burning odor of Black Camp Stove Polish on Hirschvogel.

Hirschvogel was my secret name for our big black heating stove. No one else knew it by that name. I got it from a story in my third reader about a little boy and his stove, which he nicknamed Hirschvogel. Hard times forced his family to sell Hirschvogel to buy food. The little boy was so disappointed he crawled inside the stove. When the buyer opened the door, he found the boy all sooty and black. After the lad explained how he loved the stove, the new owner gladly gave it back.

I had no real fears that we would have to sell our Hirschvogel. But should that time come, I clung to the hope that there would be a happy ending for us, too.

But back to the stove polish. When it was time to "put up the stove," a neighbor or two would help Dad move it from the corner where it had stood all summer, draped in an old bedspread. Next the stovepipes were fitted, and finally a coat of polish was applied.

If a warm blanket means security to all the Linuses of our day, then Hirschvogel spelled security for me during the long, cold winters of the thirties. This big warm stove, with chrome fittings, bell-like draft controls, and twelve tiny celluloid windows through which you could watch the fire, was almost like a person. It was my brother. We were inseparable friends seven months out of the year.

In cold weather we heated only three rooms—the kitchen, dining-sitting room, and living room. The two bedrooms were closed off until an hour before bedtime, when we might open one bedroom door "to knock the chill off."

Our heating stove was the center of home life. Families lost a great deal with the coming of central heat. When everyone clustered around a single stove, there was a togetherness not found when heat is evenly distributed through every room.

So there was a psychological as well as a physical warmth to Hirschvogel. Even the cat would crawl all the way under the warm stove, and on cold nights it took a broom to dislodge him.

Since our stove meant so much, a main concern each summer was to "lay in" the winter's coal. This wasn't easy. Although coal was cheap in Southern Illinois during the Depression, it wasn't free. Some years, Dad would trade a few days' work for a load, maybe out at Stroud's strip mine near Spillertown. Or paint a house for a trucker, who would pay with five tons of coal. One fall he borrowed a horse and wagon and hauled the coal himself. Another winter my diary reads that we got "a relief order for coal."

Filling the coal house in September afforded a real feeling of security. The big black chunks were heavy to carry and dirty to handle, but they spelled a crackling fire in January. And although a campaign slogan in 1932 promised that "The winter will be warmer with Roosevelt and Horner," we preferred to depend on Hirschvogel for that.

Hirschvogel occasionally generated excitement, such as when we burned the soot out of the stovepipes. To do this, we got the stove so hot that the soot would catch fire and fly out the chimney. Since we had wooden shingles, we chose a rainy day, when the roof was wet. But if the soot caught fire accidentally, it was like a general alarm, with each of us manning his station. Mom controlled the damper, while Dad hurriedly closed the drafts and cautiously opened the stove door to slow the force of the blaze, and I ran outside to watch for sparks on the roof. Fortunately, we never had a fire—but we did have lots of excitement!

Hirschvogel blazed away about three feet from one end of the room, leaving just enough space for a snug pallet. Words cannot express the warmth and security of the little world created by a pallet of homemade quilts in back of the stove. All of us took turns, at one time or another, napping there. As a very small boy I kept my Tinkertoys, blocks, and other equipment behind the stove. The legs of Hirschvogel were the giant supports of my own private parking garage for my little cars and trucks.

We entertained company around Hirschvogel, and here I listened to everything from neighborhood gossip to warning of world collapse because Roosevelt was trying to pack the Supreme Court.

Hirschvogel sometimes doubled as a cook stove for such chores as warming up leftovers. Here was always a teakettle; often a big pot of homemade vegetable soup or a kettle of navy beans and ham bone would be found simmering on its steady fire.

Winter bedtime came as early as seven-thirty or eight. But after *Lum and Abner* signed off there was still time for Mom to bring out a dish of apples. Or we might crack

a pan of walnuts or hickory nuts and, sitting around the
stove, pick and eat the goodies. Sometimes, in late afternoon, Mom would let the fire burn down to a bright glow
and fill the wire popper with popcorn. Holding the long,
wooden handle, she would slowly swish it back and forth
a few inches above the smoldering coals. Swish . . .
swish . . . swish . . . pop . . . swish . . . pop, pop
. . . swish swish swish . . . pop pop pop pop . . .
swish pop swish pop pop swish . . . swish pop pop . . .
swishpopswishpoppoppoppoppoppop . . . pop pop . . .
pop . . . pop . . . pop pop . . . . . p o p.

When we filled the coal buckets each afternoon, one
was for "bedding the fire." We put "slack" (tiny bits of
coal, almost dust-like) into the bottom of that bucket and
topped it with a big chunk. Near bedtime, Dad let the
fire die down before dumping in the slack. Otherwise the
fire would blaze up and burn itself out before morning.

The process was to semi-smother the fire with an even
layer of slack, then put in the big chunk. The chunk
would smolder all night and burst into flame when the
draft was opened in the morning. Occasionally Hirschvogel would "blow up," scattering soot and ashes every-
where. So Dad made sure the stove was cool enough to
take the slack without blowing up.

Before jumping into a cold bed in a refrigerated bedroom, I often held my pillow close to the fire. Or Mom
would warm a blanket to tuck me in with. If we had gone
somewhere, and came home at bedtime on a cold night,
we didn't heat up the stove, for it would take another
hour to cool down for bedding. This meant you didn't
get a warm blanket.

Bedding the fire was one of three bedtime rituals for
Dad. The second was winding the Seth Thomas clock on
the kitchen shelf. "Remember to run it up five minutes,
Eldon," Mom would remind him, a habit which started

back in 1910 when they got the clock as a premium with Larkin products. That clock still runs, and today, in its sixty-first year, when I wound it, I dutifully ran it up the five minutes it loses every twenty-four hours.

Dad's third ritual was checking the weather. "Think I'll step outside for a breath of fresh air." If the weather was clear, he might stay several minutes. Other nights he barely opened the door before a blast of arctic air drove him back.

Once inside, he gave a nightly report. "Clearin' off in the north . . . wind's shifted to the east . . . startin' to snow . . . big snow by morning . . . beginnin' to sprinkle . . . stars sure bright tonight . . . lightnin' in the west . . . cloudin' up in the southwest . . . moderatin' . . . cold rain . . . wind's pickin' up . . ."

We had a keen interest in the weather, and the first item Mom read in the paper was the forecast. She liked the fall and winter, and would write on the calendar, "first snow today," or "big snow," or "second big snow." Dad preferred the spring and summer. But in any season the changing weather was as much a part of our lives as changing sheets on the beds.

So with the fire bedded, the clock wound, and the weather forecast, we were ready for sleep. It was a simple life. But it was a good one.

BILLY ROBERTS

The carefree days of boyhood have little connection with worries over dollars and cents. The Depression may have denied me some of the frills of growing up, but it didn't rob me of the fun of just being a boy with my friends, chief of whom was Billy Roberts.

Billy lived just a block away, at 1409 N. State. "I'm going down to Billy's," I said to Mom a dozen times a day, never asking permission, for it was understood that his house and yard were the same as ours. And just as often, he told his mother, "I'm going to Bobby's."

Mr. Roberts had steadier work in the Depression, and among other luxuries they had a car. Since Billy was their only child, Mr. and Mrs. Roberts accepted me as their own. Mr. Roberts would take me and Dad and Billy fishing, with our lunches of bacon sandwiches, or swimming at the Johnston City pool.

Riding home from Johnston City—all of six miles—in the back seat of the car, with the summer wind blowing in our wet hair, Billy and I would munch away at a big Powerhouse candy bar—the ultimate in summer joy!

Mr. Roberts liked meat, especially pork chops, and the days he worked at the mines, Mrs. Roberts started frying pork chops about three in the afternoon, as they always ate early. Somehow I came to associate pork chops with prosperity, and still, when I smell pork chops frying, my first reaction is that they must be for someone else— someone who can afford meat on week nights.

Our favorite games were Monopoly in winter and mumblety-peg in summer.

Hour after hour in December and January we would play Monopoly, with the stacks of play money as real as if we were officers of the Chase Manhattan Bank. Boardwalk, Park Place, and Pennsylvania Avenue were as familiar as the streets in our own neighborhood—State and McLaren and Glendale and Logan. And the B&O and the Reading railroads were as much a part of us as the Illinois Central and the Chicago and Eastern Illinois railroads that went through Marion.

Mumblety-peg was played with a pocket knife, prefer-ably on a smooth, grassy spot. You sat facing each other, with legs spread apart, taking turns, and the first to finish won. The object was to throw the knife into the ground from about twenty-five different positions and have it stick in such a way that you could get at least two fingers between the blade and the ground.

The first maneuver was to hold the knife in the palm of your hand, blade pointed out. Then you flipped the knife over and made it come down straight so as to stick. When you missed, the other fellow took his turn.

The second maneuver was to flip the knife from the back of your hand. Then from a resting position on your right fist, then your left. Next, holding the knife between the thumb and forefinger of your right hand, you threw it six successive times into the ground. Then, balancing the tip of the knife on your left elbow, you flipped it over with your right hand—then the same trick with the right elbow.

This maneuver was then executed from both shoulders. Next, you threw the knife backwards over your left shoulder, then your right shoulder, and finally over your head, to land on the dirt behind you. Now the hard part, where you held your right ear with your left hand, extended your right hand through the circle thus formed, and flipped the knife to the ground. Then reversed, holding your left ear with your right hand.

The most dangerous trick was to hold the knife flat against your forehead with the palm of your right hand, blade pointed up through your hair. With a quick out and down flip, you (hopefully) plummeted the knife into the ground. Next, using your left hand, you made a "fence," placed the knife slantwise in the ground, and with your right hand flipped it up and over the "fence," hoping it landed upright.

This brought you to the final maneuver. Balancing the knife on your right thumb, blade down, you flipped the knife off and into the ground. This you repeated with all four fingers, saying aloud, "O-U-T-SPELLS-OUT!"

For real action, nothing could substitute for a good game of Cowboys'n'Indians. With an arsenal of cap pistols, rubber guns, water guns, pop guns, belt and holster sets with "real" wooden bullets, wooden guns, Indian feather headdresses, fringed pants, cowboy hats, bandanas, and homemade bows and arrows, we could roll back the calendar from 1930 to 1830 as quickly as you could tie a red bandana around your neck. And believe me when I say it wasn't make-believe. It was real!

You learned to run in a gallop, and to grab your chest with a jerk when you were "shot," hanging momentarily in the air, then slowly falling in a heap to the ground. A good 'game of Cowboys'n'Indians would cover several blocks of the neighborhood, with herds of buffaloes and Indians on wild pintos cutting across open lots, up the alleys, and down the streets.

Spring would soon bring out the marbles. You always made sure you had at least one "shootin' tall" [taw], although it wasn't fair to shoot with a "steelie," a little steel marble that could shatter a "glassie" with a direct hit. Whether you played for "keeps" or for fun depended on the skill of your opponent.

In March we made kites out of newspapers or brown wrapping paper, flour paste, and strips of rags for tails. On summer nights we played "Release," again ranging over several blocks, with rival teams of as many as fifteen or twenty kids. Or maybe street hockey, using tin cans creased in the middle. Or before dark, "Handy Over," a simple game of throwing a sponge or tennis ball over the house and then running around to tag the person on the other side before he caught the ball.

If we turned to Cops'n'Robbers, we changed, for some reason, to rubber guns. These were homemade wooden

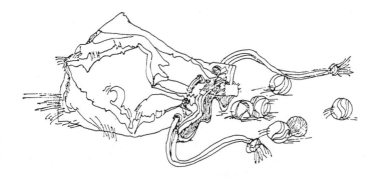

gun stalks, with a spring-type clothes pin that released the taut rings of rubber made from old inner tubes. The longer the gun barrel and the thinner the rubber rings, the farther they traveled and the harder they stung. Maybe we thought that if we were going to imitate John Dillinger we needed live ammunition, whereas for Billy the Kid we were satisfied with toy guns.

We also made slingshots from inner tubes and forked limbs, and homemade scooters with two boards and the wheels off an old roller skate.

With old tires, you could roll up inside while a friend pushed you down a hill. Or you could just roll a tire down the street for the fun of it. Or with opposing teams, each soldier armed with a tire, you could play "war," sending the tires crashing into each other, seeing which side could knock the others down first.

One summer a group of us made a "swing for your life" between two big trees on an empty lot. One end of a steel cable was fastened to a high limb of one tree and the other end to the bottom of the trunk of the other tree. A six-inch length of water pipe was threaded over the cable, and boards were nailed horizontally on the one tree so you could climb to the high end of the cable. First you rubbed your hands in the dust to dry the sweat, lest you lose your grip. Then, grasping the pipe in both hands, you pushed off and slid hilariously, if not precariously, down the length of the cable, turning loose just before you slammed into the anchor tree.

Sitting on the curb under the streetlight was another summertime favorite. The old-fashioned street lamp, consisting of a single incandescent bulb, cast only a small circle of light underneath, highlighting the darkness and shadows. Telling ghost stories in the pale, yellow glow of a streetlight made it scary to walk home by yourself. But no one dared to admit fear, and each tried to outdo the other when it came his time to recite a horror tale.

Most of the games we played were our own, and cost almost nothing.

The Roberts family moved when we were teenagers, and we saw little of each other afterwards. The last I heard from Billy was a Christmas card in December of 1944. At the bottom he penned, "Bob don't forget me."

On May 11, 1945, he was killed by a Japanese kami- kaze plane which crashed on the deck of the aircraft car- rier *Bunker Hill*, just off Okinawa. He was buried at sea, and his parents erected a marker in the Rose Hill Ceme- tery in Marion.

Even if he hadn't asked, I couldn't forget him, any more than a man can forget the make-believe, fun-filled, never-never days of his boyhood.

A LIGHT AT BILLY'S HOUSE

"Get up, Bobby. There's already a light at Billy's." Although it was only three A.M., I didn't need coaxing. This was the day of the state band contest at Bloomington. For months we had dreamed of that special train pulling into the Illinois Central station on North Market Street. Now we were within minutes of actual departure. Billy Roberts' father would drive the two of us to the station.

The four years I played in the Marion Grade School Band were as far from the Depression as the birds that sang in our two big maple trees. A band instrument was your ticket to all kinds of exciting trips, contests, parades, fairs, and free meals and treats.

I had wanted to play some instrument since I first stood on a footstool to crank our old-fashioned upright victrola. After putting on a favorite record, perhaps a march by Sousa, I would turn in my imagination to a vast audience and "direct" the band with a make-believe baton.

When I was in the fifth grade, Gordon, my oldest brother, bought me a brand new B-flat clarinet from J. B. Heyde & Sons. I say "brand new" with pride. This was no Depression hand-me-down. It even smelled new!

When I opened the black case, there lay this silver, glistening horn in rich, red velvet. It was a Midas-like treasure.

Like so many teenagers during the Depression, Gordon traded high school for hunting work in Chicago. Glenn Travelstead, a family friend and cousin by marriage, also from Southern Illinois, was bell captain at the old Manger Hotel. If he could, Glenn gave jobs to boys from Marion and Herrin and Harrisburg. When a vacancy occurred, the manager would say, "Glenn, get me another bellhop from Southern Illinois. They're not like these Chicago boys. They know how to work." Gordon became one of those lucky boys.

Whenever he wrote home, Gordon enclosed one or two dollar bills. Or maybe a fifty-cent piece wrapped in tissue paper. That little trickle of cash seemed like a river. And when he sent thirty-five dollars for my clarinet—well, that was unbelievable.

Band director George Ashley was a legend in Marion. He lived from one spring contest to the next, never failing to lead a winning band. He planned it that way.

He went from school to school giving individual lessons. Then on Monday, Tuesday, Wednesday, and Thursday afternoons, kids from all over town walked to the old Washington School on West Jefferson Street for band practice. In winter it was not uncommon to walk home by moonlight, as rehearsals could last until five-thirty or six.

I was too excited to know even the day of the week when I carried my new clarinet to the Jefferson School on East Boulevard for my first lesson. I was too spellbound to hear a word Mr. Ashley said.

Presumably, he taught me to finger C, D, E, F, and G, using the thumb and the first three fingers of the left hand. But at home, when I tried to practice, I couldn't finger a single note.

A week later Mr. Ashley, knitting his fierce, bushy eyebrows, said, "Bobby, I can't waste my time if you can't learn even one note a week." I was crushed. But he patiently reviewed how to play C, D, E, F, and G with the three fingers and the thumb of your left hand.

Six weeks later he said, "Come to band practice Monday." All the victrolas in Marion started playing at once!

Perhaps the best-known band member was Tony Mazzara, only slightly larger than his tiny E-flat clarinet. Tony's dad was the hot tamale man of Marion. He was a familiar figure on the streets on windy, cold nights, shouting, "Hot tamales, hot tamales, get 'em while they're hot." In summers he drove a little pony-pulled ice cream wagon around town.

Ashley believed the more exposure we got to crowds, the greater our self-confidence would be at contest time. So he never missed a chance for us to play at the Rotary and Lions clubs (free dinner) and between features at the Orpheum Theater (free tickets).

For band trips, we usually took a bus. Marion had no school buses, but Courtney Moving and Storage Company operated one or two buses here and there. One made a daily round trip to Carbondale during the school year. College students caught the bus as it meandered around Marion, rode to Southern Illinois Normal University for classes, and returned home at night.

When time came for the district contest in Carbondale, we chartered one of Courtney's buses for the seventeen-mile trip. The bus parked at one corner of the tiny campus, and we marched over to Shryock Auditorium. When the schedule called for the Marion band to play its three numbers, we strutted confidently onto the stage. And although Shryock looked as big as Madison Square Garden, we showed little fear. For after all, hadn't we played at the Orpheum Theater in Marion, with real spotlights on Mr. Ashley? The boy sitting next to me, Bill D. Hudgens, was later to hold a prominent position on the university's staff.

But the year of years was the one in which we rode the special train to Bloomington for the state contest. That was no ordinary train. The Illinois Central had spotted coaches all over Southern Illinois. The engine, two coaches, and a baggage car originated at Marion about four A.M. At each town we stopped to hook on another car.

"Now you kids listen," Ashley warned. "Stay in the Marion car. Don't be running up and down the train. Get a little sleep. If you get to Bloomington too tired to play, I'll never take you anywhere again."

He might as well have told the soot blowing out from the coal-burning engines to stay in the boilers.

At each stop we got off to see the next car being added. By the time we reached Bloomington, that I.C. train was one, two, maybe three miles long!

Word soon spread up and down the coaches that the rivalry between Marion and Carbondale and West Frankfort and DuQuoin would not be settled on the concert platform at Bloomington, but in a war of waterguns. Some had brought guns from home. Others tried to buy them at stops enroute. The dime stores in Bloomington sold out.

When our train finally rolled back into Marion about twenty-four hours later, there was still a light at Billy's house. His dad met us. As we drove home in the predawn darkness, it didn't seem nearly so important who had won first or second or third—what counted was who had come out best in the Battle of the Dime Store Waterguns.

THREE BALLS AND NO HITS

The climax of each summer was the Williamson County Fair. It usually began the week before Labor Day, and school always dismissed on Thursday and Friday.

We had no uniform pattern for attending the Fair, except that when we went as a family, it was always on Thursday, which was Republican Day. Friday was Democrat Day, which we avoided as something resembling the seven-year itch.

The amusement rides, bingo game tents, frozen custard stand, and other concessions started going up on

Sunday. Since the gate was free until Wednesday, half the fun was going out on Monday or Tuesday to see what you were going to enjoy on Thursday!

Once or twice we made a day of it, taking a basket lunch which we spread in the centerfield under the big oak trees. Other years I went alone.

A big deal was sitting in the yard of Dad's two aunts, Dialtha James and Mary Roberts, who lived across from the fairgrounds, at 306 N. Fair. In the early thirties some fairgoers still came in buggies and wagons. Great numbers walked. So we sat watching the stream of humanity pass, a show in itself. Also, it was big sport to watch the "fence-jumpers" to see if they made it.

One or two years, Dad worked as a guard and was assigned a stretch of fence to patrol. He was issued a walking cane and a flat-brimmed straw hat. The chief pay was a free family pass.

The fence fell into disrepair during the Depression, with scores of palings broken off, making it easy for the gate-crashers to slip in, under, or over. I suppose it was cheaper for the Fair Board to hire guards than to patch the fence.

If anything, the guards were more sympathetic with those who wanted to sneak in than with the Fair Board. Dad would tell his friends that when they were ready to "go over," he would look the other way. This was so common a practice that no one seemed to feel it was dishonest. It reflected a camaraderie of the Depression in which you felt an obligation to help everyone else.

Still, an occasional culprit would be "caught" by a guard. Although the only penalty was to be turned back, we who were watching would cry out, "There, he got one!" It was about as much fun watching who got caught and who didn't as it was seeing the bearded lady in one of the side shows. We always rooted for the "bad" guys who were slipping in.

One year Dad got permission to park cars in my aunts' yard for ten cents a car, and they agreed to split the proceeds. He stood in the street with a walking cane, flagging would-be customers. But most people would rather drive a half mile to find free parking than pay as little as a dime.

A big steel-and-concrete grandstand faced the race track and stage, where afternoon and night stage shows were given by clowns, magicians, and trapeze artists. You had to buy a ticket to sit there. On either side were two smaller, wooden grandstands, little more than bleachers with a roof. They were usually dirty and littered, and you had to strain to see the stage show. I remember sitting in the free wooden stands, looking across at the pay grandstand, and imagining what it might be like to sit in a reserved seat and buy red soda from the hawkers.

One September, in the worst of the Depression, I went to the Fair alone. As a family, we didn't even go over to

Aunt Dialtha's to watch the fence-jumpers. But Mom and Dad set aside 25¢ for me.

"Now you can ride one of the swings for a dime some time in the afternoon, use a nickel to buy you a pop or a frozen custard about three o'clock, and then have a dime for your lemonade and hamburger at supper," Mom explained. She also listed other ways the quarter could be budgeted, leaving me to choose how I would actually spend it.

I took the first hour sizing up the rides. Should I spend the dime on the Ferris wheel? Or the merry-go-round, which gave the added bonus of lively music? Or the chair swing, which consisted of about thirty wooden chairs or swings attached to long chains, which swung around in a big circle so you could imagine you were taking off in an airplane, then coming in for a landing. Or maybe the caterpillar, a string of little cars which went round and round on an up-and-down track, looking much like a real caterpillar, especially when the green tarpaulin covers snapped shut, making the inside dark and spooky.

"A quarter's just not enough to go to the Fair on," I told myself. Then I drifted over to the Sock-It-To-'Em stand, where for a nickel you could buy three baseballs to throw at a pyramid of six clay milk bottles. If you downed all six, you got a quarter. "Now if I spend a nickel for three balls, I'll have 20¢ left, plus my winning 25¢, making 45¢ in all," I reasoned. It looked like a sure thing.

To my dismay, after aiming my best with all three balls, I hit only one or two bottles.

I put down another nickel. No hits. And another nickel. No hits.

Now I had only a dime left. One ride, or a drink and a sandwich. I turned away dejected.

In a few minutes I ran into my friend, Billy Roberts. "Let's ride on the Ferris wheel," he cried. I told him my plight.

"My Daddy will take care of that," he boasted. And sure enough, Mr. Roberts gave me a handful of coins, enough for a couple of rides, a frozen custard, and my supper.

We stayed through the night stage show, and even though we sat in the dusty wooden bleachers, I felt like the luckiest boy in Williamson County. Someone up there, I concluded, must surely be looking after me.

It was my best Fair, and my last try at knocking over clay milk bottles.

DR. CALDWELL'S SYRUP OF PEPSIN

Except for the brief illness of my brother which resulted in his death, we kept remarkably healthy during the Depression. Both Mom and Dad were in their seventies before either was a hospital patient. All four of us children were born at home, with the simplest of medical care.

Since a hospital was a place where you went to die, or to have an operation for appendicitis, and since there was no hospital in Marion anyway, our energies were directed toward staying well.

When we did get sick, home remedies were the rule.

For bandaids, Mom kept a supply of white cotton cloth salvaged from shirts or sheets. These homemade bandages were tied with cotton string or thin strips of the same material.

You put the back of your hand to someone's forehead to test for fever. And if he had a temperature, a wet cloth was laid across his forehead.

Warm, salt water made a good gargle, or was used to bathe your eyes if they were sore, red, or burning. Sores were sometimes bathed in salt water, too. If a cut or sore itched, it was getting well.

Arm and Hammer bicarbonate of soda also served as a gargle for sore throat, an eye wash, a dentifrice, and a remedy for upset stomach, burns, or insect bites.

Epsom Salts ("Ma took salts all her life," Mom used to say) was a good laxative, or "purgative" as we called it, as well as a remedy for rheumatism.

Mom also put a great deal of faith in Vicks salve. She often quoted an old friend who, years earlier, had said, "If I had pneumonia, I would as soon go to bed with a bottle of Vicks salve as anything I know of."

That simple testimony was often quoted as gospel, so we used Vicks for chapped hands and lips, insect bites, and colds. For a cold, you sniffed it in your nose, which "loosened up your head." At night Mom rubbed Vicks on my chest, then warmed an old piece of flannel or wool next to the heating stove, fastened it to my underwear, finally pinning my blanket to the mattress so I wouldn't "fan around while you're asleep and catch more cold."

But we could never remember whether to starve a fever and feed a cold, or starve a cold and feed a fever. So we usually ate what we wanted when we wanted it.

Dad often asked me to stick out my tongue to see if it was coated. There were three signs of "puniness" in a boy: a coated tongue, white around the mouth, or circles under the eyes.

We were never without a big bottle of Dr. Caldwell's Syrup of Pepsin, and at the first sign of "puniness," I was given a big tablespoonful at bedtime. I liked the taste so much I would have feigned "puniness" to get some.

Regardless of other remedies, Mom believed that every growing boy needed an occasional dose of castor oil, especially in the spring. One entry in my diary reads, "Went

to the doctor. Gave me worm medicine, then castor oil
for three days."

If a fellow wasn't weak from a case of the worms, he
needn't worry. He would be after three days of castor oil.

However, there was a bright side, for I went to Swan's
Store with a nickel for a bottle of orange soda. This was
my "reward," and while I was downing the castor oil,
gagging and struggling, Mom imitated a barker at the
county fair, "Here, here, get your red lemonade over
here . . . ice cold . . . sweet as honey . . . come on,
come on, only a nickel for a big, frosty glass . . ."

The sound effects helped, but castor oil is still castor
oil.

One winter my right eye swelled and got inflamed.
Thinking it could be serious, Dad took me to a specialist
after school. It took about three minutes. The doctor
said it was a simple sty and gave me a little can of salve.

Dad asked the charge, for it was customary to pay in
cash.

"Five dollars," the doctor replied.

Dad hesitated. Based on our income, that was three days' pay. Then he reached into his pocket for the money.

We walked home in silence, taking a short cut down the IC tracks, past the "Hoover Hotel," the big IC water tower, which was a favorite overnight stop for tramps during the Depression. Here they huddled around an open fire, heating soup and coffee in tin cans. The forlorn men who kept on the move during the thirties, riding in boxcars, begging at back doors, and drinking coffee out of tin cans, were always a source of amazement to me. They seemed harmless enough, but when I passed the "Hoover Hotel" I always walked on the opposite side of the track.

A little way on, Dad and I turned left from the tracks and took another shortcut along the city reservoir. Why I can pinpoint my feelings to a particular stretch of gravel path beside that reservoir I don't know. But the memory is as vivid as was that winter afternoon in 1935.

I wanted to reach up and take Dad's hand and say how sorry I was that three days' pay had gone so fast. I wanted to say that five dollars was too much. But words would not match my feelings.

I am not saying that the eye, ear, nose, and throat specialist overcharged us. Maybe there were hours that day when he didn't have a single patient. I'm just trying to say how much it hurt. But I can't, any more than I could then.

TED'S LAST DIME

Ted Boles reached into his pocket and pulled out a dime. "Fellows," he said, speaking to the men and boys sprawled out on his lawn at 1200 N. Logan on a summer

Saturday evening, "this is my last dime. And tomorrow I'm going to spend it for a *St. Louis Globe*."

The major topic of conversation at this family get-together, as it was so often in the thirties, was the Depression. Ted Boles had married Dad's niece, Flossie Hastings, and theirs was one of about a dozen families with whom we visited back and forth during the Depression, taking dinner with one this Sunday, with another the next. Or dropping in on Saturday night to play dominoes and make divinity or popcorn balls.

"Visiting" was our chief diversion, and it cost very little. But its rewards were rich. Family ties, on both Dad's and Mom's side of the family, bound us together when each had so little by himself, but so much of warmth and friendship with each other.

Ted was not lying when he said it was his last dime. I'm sure it was, for that week. But the next week he would haul someone a load of coal in his truck, or work a day or two in one of the "gopher" mines between Marion and Harrisburg.

As far as I was concerned, I couldn't have been happier than to hear him say he was going to buy a paper with that dime, for a Sunday paper meant getting to read the funnies.

We seldom bought a Sunday paper during the Depression, but two or three families in the neighborhood did. I knew that Ted would buy the *Globe*, his brother-in-law Archie Rodd would get a *Chicago Tribune*, and Walter Lang was good for a *St. Louis Post-Dispatch*.

Each of these families was kind enough to save the funnies for me. If I didn't drop by on Sunday afternoon, I could still go Monday after school. Those were the days of *Moon Mullins*, *Bringing Up Father*, *The Katzenjammer Kids*, *Gasoline Alley*, *Little Orphan Annie*, *Flash Gordon*, *Tillie the Toiler*, *Blondie*, *Out Our Way*, and *Born 30 Years Too Soon*.

On Dad's side, we also took dinner frequently with his Aunt Dialtha and Aunt Mary, who lived together on North Fair Street. Like many people of that day, they actually had two sitting or living rooms, one of which had a fireplace that was opened only for company. Over the fireplace was a picture of a winter scene in a small village, with bright lights from a church reflecting on the snow, and a couple driving up in a fancy sled pulled by a prancing, spirited horse.

It was just another picture, but when I went there I couldn't take my eyes away from it. Maybe it was just a childhood fascination; maybe it was awe of a day when people dressed in fine furs and laughed as they rode through the snow.

Mealtime at the home of Annie and John Sharp, Dad's sister and her husband, stands out in my memory because of the grace she always offered. Reared a Baptist, she joined the growing Penecostal movement in the late twenties, attracted by what she called "real spiritual religion." A deeply sincere woman, she always closed her prayer with a long sigh. Then, under her breath, barely whispering, "Precious Jesus, bless his name . . . bless his h-o-l-y name." Finally another sigh, this time deeper than ever. That was the final signal to "reach and help yourselves, and if you don't see what you want, just ask."

I must say a word about Link and Etta Hartwell, who lived in a big house at 1701 W. Main which they rented as two apartments, living themselves in the basement. Link had a steady job throughout the Depression —he worked nights for forty-five years for the Peabody Coal Company. Etta was dietitian at the high-school cafeteria.

Etta liked good food, and she enjoyed entertaining and being entertained. Mom thought of her as a "fancy" cook because she specialized in unusual salads, and she had expensive silverware and crystal.

"Ruby," she would say to Mom, "Link and I went out to eat last Sunday and I got me a shrimp cocktail."

I had never seen a shrimp cocktail. The only cocktail I knew anything about was an alcoholic drink, and the only shrimp I had seen was any pint-sized fellow you could push around.

Etta also had an electric liquefier, the only one I had ever seen. They made drinks out of radishes, onions, carrots, potatoes, and anything else that could be liquefied. Link, especially, had a mania for those fresh juices. They evidently helped him, for he worked until he was seventy-eight and lived to be eighty-seven.

Mom always felt a little self-conscious cooking for the Hartwells. Yet our relatives knew that Mom always outcooked Etta. Mom may not have had the fancy salads and crystal goblets, but from her garden and pantry, the relief orders, or fresh meat brought by her sisters at butchering time, she put a meal together in a way that made shrimp cocktail look like a warmed-over hamburger.

And if you watched Etta closely at a family potluck, she always reached for Mom's dishes first.

THE ONE-DOLLAR BICYCLE

"Bob, you can fix that tire by pouring a can of Pet Milk through the valve stem," my cousin Kenneth Rodd told me as I started pushing my "new" bicycle home.

Kenneth and his brother Charles, who had won a new, brown and gold Ranger bicycle with real balloon tires by selling subscriptions to the *St. Louis Post-Dispatch*, sold me their old one.

It was a big, unsightly thirty-inch relic with tubeless tires, but it was for real, and after all, it cost only one

dollar. Except for that back tire. It had a slow leak, and
you couldn't patch it. And you couldn't buy a tube, because it was tubeless. And you couldn't go buy a $1.50
tire for a $1 bicycle.

I remember two things about the Pet Milk. It didn't
work. And the stink of sour canned milk inside a tire
takes a long time to go away.

Since the leak was a slow one, I compromised by pushing the bike to the filling station each morning for free
air.

A bicycle in a small town gives a boy tremendous mo-
bility. It puts him in instant touch with whatever goes
on, whether he's following the fire truck to a blaze,
wheeling out to the county fairgrounds to watch the
workmen put up the rides, going down to the IC station
to see the circus unload, or riding over to the city park to
watch a Sunday afternoon free baseball game.

A bicycle that cost only $1, with the paint scratched
off and one tire about gone, had another advantage. You

didn't have to be too careful. You could jump curbs. You could ride through puddles of water and mud, holding your legs up and letting the water splash where it would. You could imitate the daredevil auto drivers at the county fair by jumping off mounds of cinders in the schoolyard, trying to see who could jump his bike the farthest. Or you could slam the brakes on hard and slide the rear wheel around in a cloud of dust, or ride with no hands, taking a curve by leaning your weight in the direction you wanted to go.

Since we had no car during the Depression, I was the family errand boy, going to the store for small orders, paying the light bill, or stopping by the Metropolitan office to pay our two insurance policies—one for 10¢ a week and one for 69¢ a month.

A big catalpa tree stood in the corner of Walter Lang's yard across the street, and one August afternoon a group of us boys decided to make homemade smokes out of its dry leaves and beans.

Equipped with cigarette papers, matches, and crushed beans, we rode over to the C&EI tracks near Rose Hill Cemetery. C&EI stood for Chicago and Eastern Illinois railroad, only the way we ran the letters together, I was almost grown before I realized it wasn't the "*Seen*-E-I."

Anyway, while we were trying to roll those ground-up catalpa beans, someone struck a match and dropped it in the dry grass along the tracks. We tried to stamp out the blaze with our bare feet, but the wind fanned it out of control, and it raced up the bank toward the cemetery.

Now if you really wanted to set a brush fire in Marion, say, just for the fun of it, you certainly didn't start it in Rose Hill Cemetery! That's where some benefactor by the name of Goddard had built a little English-style chapel. It gave a lot of class to the cemetery, and the fact that the chapel was seldom used added to the extravagance of having built it in the first place.

Seeing the fire race out of hand, and not wishing to answer any questions, we mounted our bikes for home. Only we didn't go the direct route down East De Young and then north on State. Instead, we rode south to Boulevard, turned east as far as Garfield, then north on Garfield, and then home. This meant we reached our neighborhood from the east. The fire was in the west.

Mom was in the back yard, watching the smoke.

"Looks like a pretty big fire," she said.

"Yes."

"Seems to be over by the cemetery. You don't suppose Rose Hill could be on fire?"

"Surely not."

As the sirens pierced the still, hot afternoon, I bounded up the back porch steps in a diversionary tactic.

"I'm hungry. Anything left from dinner?"

"Yes. There's some sweet 'taters with the jackets in the oven."

THE SCAVENGER MAN

The Depression caught a number of families in Marion with their pants down—that is, in outdoor toilets. Most of these drafty, unpainted two-holers were near the edges of town, but an occasional one could be spotted in nearly every neighborhood. Except Parrish Park, the silk-stocking southeast corner of town.

Ours sat at the back of our lot, just next to the alley. On summer nights I was often awakened by a creaking wagon making its way down the alley, a couple of kerosene lanterns swaying fore and aft.

"Whoa there, whoa . . . back up, you good-for-nothin' critter," the driver called out in the still night, as he tried to maneuver the "honey" wagon close to the toilets. Then he would shovel the contents into his wagon, leaving two neat holes for next month's waste.

"They're too triflin' to pay the scavenger man" was about the meanest thing you could say about a family. "If he was a mind to," the scavenger man could pass up non-paying customers. But neighborhood pressure had a way of building up when the July heat triggered offensive odors and swarms of flies, and by the next month most "triflin' " families got hold of at least fifty cents to pay the scavenger man.

Standard toilet paper was a catalog, and if you were careful, the spring-and-summer catalog would last until the fall-and-winter issue. But catalogs lost popularity when Sears and Montgomery Ward printers began using more and more slick-finish color pages.

"Bringing in the slop jar" was a pre-bedtime ritual, usually reserved until after dark. The utensil was also called the "chamber" or "chamber pot." That old speckled, grey-blue pot, slightly curved near the top, with a matching lid, a wire bail, and a wooden handle, was a crude form of indoor plumbing that came in real handy in cold weather and during sickness. A midnight trip to the outhouse on a zero night cured you of sleepy-headedness, but it could give you something worse in its stead.

"Emptying the slop jar" was a morning ritual usually performed before breakfast. Then the pot was rinsed at the well with clear water and, in summer, left exposed to the sunlight or, in winter, returned to the house. We had never heard of hepatitis and fortunately never took it, at least to our knowledge.

During the Depression, men on WPA constructed outdoor sanitary toilets, and the name "WPA toilet" still identifies a certain style. But ours was neither sanitary nor WPA. It was just outdoors. And believe me, more out than in.

"Tipping toilets" on Halloween night reached a height of popularity when my brothers were teenagers. Usually only one or two toilets in any one neighborhood were tipped. But there was always a good deal of apprehension over whose turn it might be this year, for most of the buildings were rather flimsy and if pushed over with any force were likely to collapse in a cloud of dust and splinters.

Fortunately, ours was never tipped, since the boys who participated in this nocturnal sport would usually bypass houses where other teenagers lived. With this "protection" our little house survived Halloween as well as wind and time.

Teenage boys in our neighborhood were more numerous when I was a pre-schooler than when I reached the teens. By the time I was old enough for Halloween "monkeyshines," the big sport was "chatting" porches. You put your costume over your overalls and went door to door. Not to trick or treat, but to stand in awkward silence as the neighbors tried to guess who you were.

Before starting out, you found a driveway with very fine chat (gravel) and filled your overall pockets. You also carried a bar of soap. While inside a home, you held the bar of soap behind you and smeared windows, mirrors, or painted doors. Once outside, you threw a barrage of chat across the porch. Fine chat, thrown evenly across a porch, sounded just like hail, and a few pebbles always glanced harmlessly off the front windows.

Then the porch light came on and out burst the householders, shading their eyes with their hands, peering into the darkness, and hollering, "I know who you are, and if you do that again I'm going to . . ."

But back to my brothers. When they were teenagers, a group of boys on North State and North Glendale formed their own neighborhood gang. They rustled up some old boards, some tin roofing, a pot-bellied stove, some rusted stovepipe, and some broken-down furniture, and built what they called "The Hut" in the vacant lot next door.

One of my earliest memories is of wanting to be a member and get inside that cozy hut on cold, rainy days. One day I slipped in long enough to see the rundown furnishings, the threadbare rug on the ground, and the roaring fire. To me, it was like a big hunting lodge that Robin Hood and his men might have built.

One New Year's Eve they had a party in the hut. "We're going to stay up and watch the Old Year go out," they boasted in condescending tones. Thinking the Old Year would parade down the alley at midnight like the scavenger man in summer, I begged to stay up, too.

I could imagine nothing more exciting than actually seeing the Old Year of 1928, bent and grey, shouldering his scythe, groping his way down the alley at the stroke of twelve, while the infant 1929 crawled along behind.

But I wasn't old enough to tip toilets, so I wasn't old enough to sit by the pot-bellied stove and eat potatoes roasted in the ashes and drink homemade root beer.

A WALKING NEWSPAPER

Although we canceled our subscription to the *Marion Daily Republican* when Old West Side mine shut down in 1930, we weren't cut off entirely from local news. Baby news, that is. Although the birth rate dropped dramatically during the Depression, there were still enough births in Marion to make them a lively topic of conversation.

We had one neighbor who could sense an impending visit from the stork almost before the mother herself. Her name was Lizzie Davis.

In 1909, Lizzie and Ezra Davis built a four-room house at 1314 N. Glendale, just one block from us. Later they added a couple of rooms and dug a basement. For forty years they were the closest of neighbors to my parents. Before we got our radio, each Saturday night found us at the Davis home, listening to the *Grand Ol' Opry* from WSM in Nashville, Tennessee.

Ezra, who always raised a big bed of colorful gladioli each summer, was a man of few words. He said "Yes" and he said "No." And when you've said that, you've said about all he said. I remember our walking in (we never knocked) about six on cold Saturday nights in the winter. Ezra would be making a supply of "roll your own" cigarets with a little gadget he had bought. I was always fascinated by the number of smokes he could get out of just one can of fairly inexpensive tobacco. Just as words were unnecessary for raising gladioli in the summer or rolling cigarets in the winter, so they were not wasted on us. We understood and accepted his silence. Besides, with a wife like Lizzie he didn't need to talk!

Mom called her a "walking newspaper." She knew just about everything that went on in the north end of Marion, and much that happened in the south end. We never thought of her as a gossip—she was simply interested in people. Especially babies and women "in a family way."

"Ruby," she would begin, "have you heard about . . . ?" and here she would cover the side of her mouth with her hand to keep me from hearing.

"No, I haven't heard a word. What do you mean?"

"You know what I mean."

"You don't . . . !"

"Yes, I'll swear to my soul it's true. And her with two younguns still in diapers. And he's been laid off all winter, you know."

You didn't say "pregnant" in the thirties. You said a woman was "in a family way." By the forties it was proper to say she was "expecting." But "pregnant" was too earthy, too frank, too sensual. Having a baby was something that slipped up on you. You didn't acknowledge it openly. A baby sort of drifted in, like snow under a crack in the kitchen door.

If the expectant mother already had several children, or one "still in diapers," or if she were a little past the normal childbearing years, the news traveled fast.

In 1932, the Davis' daughter and son-in-law, Lucille and Bill Russell, moved in with them, Bill having lost his job in East St. Louis. This brought the baby business right into their home, for Lucille was pregnant—oops!— "in a family way." What made it so funny was that this time it slipped up on Lizzie herself. For some reason Lucille lost weight rather dramatically during the early part of her pregnancy.

Lucille recalls that Dad would walk over to their house some mornings that summer and say, "Lizzie, there's something wrong with that girl. Better get her to a doctor."

Lucille remembers the night Shirley Mae was born, for "all the neighbor kids knew something was up when they saw Dr. Baker's car in front of our house." We sat on the curb under the streetlight, waiting for developments.

This was the closest I had been to the birth of a real, live baby, and for the life of me, I had no idea where she came from. About all I knew was that babies arrived not too long after Lizzie Davis, with a sparkle in her eyes, cupped a hand over one side of her mouth.

During the Depression, Lucille, Bill, Lizzie, and Ezra worked as paperhangers, often for as little as $1 a room. Lizzie could climb ladders like a man and slap the paper on the ceiling like a pro. Since Dad also picked up a few dollars hanging paper, they often traded ladders, pasting boards, and brushes. With no car, moving the ladders from one job to another was sometimes more of a problem than hanging the paper itself.

In the winter, Lizzie often dropped in for a visit as early as six A.M. She would sit behind the heating stove, warming her feet on the brass fittings, while we ate breakfast. This was the Depression version of the *Today* show, for we heard a varied comment on what was "comin' and goin'," including the "family way" announcements.

Each January, Mom would walk over to Lizzie's with her Wearever aluminum pan, Swan's Down cake flour, and egg beater, to bake one of her famous thirteen-egg angel food cakes for Ezra's birthday. "Now you girls stay out of the kitchen," Lizzie would warn Caroline, Lucille, and Katherine. "And don't jump or run across the floor, or you'll cause Ruby's cake to fall, and your Daddy won't have anything for his birthday."

Then, as if by magic, the cake would rise tall and majestic in the oven, white as the Swan's Down flour on the inside and brown as a suntan on the outside.

Each fall, Mom and Lizzie made apple butter outside in Lizzie's big old kettle. In August they would take turns helping each other peel peaches to can.

Lizzie's dad, W. D. Sinks, owned a peach orchard north of Spillertown. Invariably she came home with at least one bushel of soft, bruised peaches she had picked off the ground. Mom scolded her, "Now Lizzie, if you get another bushel of these overripe peaches, I'll not help you peel a single one. I can't understand why, when they are free, you don't get the best."

"You're right. I know it, I know it," Lizzie would agree good-naturedly. "But I can't stand to see all those peaches out there on the ground going to waste. They'll make good cobblers next winter, even if they are soft."

Mom always cold-packed her peaches, which means they were put in the jars raw, covered with sugar syrup, sealed, and cooked in boiling water. We would set a tub on bricks in the back yard, put rags in the bottom, fill it with water, and then build a fire under it. Then the jars were gently spaced in the tub, the cotton cloths insulating them against the hot bottom of the tub, with the water coming up to their necks. This assured firm, instead of soft and dark, fruit which resulted if the peaches were cooked before canning.

Late in the summer evening, we would carry the glass jars, still warm, into the house one by one, and set them on the cabinet. Some of the peaches were reddish, others yellow. But they all glowed with a succulent goodness and were in themselves insurance against winter hunger —a promise of rich cobblers on cold days.

TWO-PENNY LOUIE

Since allowances for kids were about as rare as jobs during the Depression, a boy looked where he could for spending money. You could always pick up milk bottles in the alley and redeem them for 2¢ in trade at the grocery. Or soft drink bottles. Only I don't recall ever seeing a stray Coke bottle in our neighborhood. Anyone lucky enough to have a nickel for a Coke drank it at the filling station.

Scrap iron you sold down at Gudder's junkyard on North Monroe, next to the IC tracks. Every old piece of metal from junk cars or wornout bicycles was saved and carried in a tow sack down to "Two-Penny Louie's."

Louie Gudder, who operated the junk yard, was said to have earned this nickname because, regardless of how

much your scrap weighed, he supposedly grunted, "Two cents."

A big man, with his belly hanging over his belt, he sat hour after hour in the shade of an old shed, waiting for scavengers to haul in junk by the truckload, gunny sack full, or a child's wagonload.

I picked up a good bit of spending money by mowing yards for two widows in our neighborhood. Mrs. Martha McCowan had a 25¢ yard and Mrs. Sena Sinks had a 15¢ yard. And in the winter I brought in Mrs. Sinks' coal and kindling and carried out her ashes for another 15¢ a week.

I always thought Mrs. Sinks had the cleanest house imaginable. I often wondered how she kept her heating stove so clean, for not a speck of ashes was anywhere to be found. Maybe it was because she worked so many years as a housekeeper for other people. She had moved her four little girls to Marion, where she could get housework, in 1918, after the death of her husband, John.

Hard-working, frugal, yet generous, she often said to Mom, "Ruby, if you will just set aside a tithe for the Lord, you'll never be without a little money." And she never was.

One summer I wrote in my diary that I made 50¢ "mowing Mrs. McCowan's lot at the cemetery." But it was a one-time job. I didn't care much, for tying the mower on the back of your bike put the blades in gear and made it hard to pull. Only if you pushed it in front of you could you turn it over and make it freewheeling.

I kept my money in a little transparent celluloid bank, shaped like a cash register, which sat in our china closet. As I grew older I gradually forgot about it. Then, on our wedding day, April 1, 1945, at the First Baptist Church in DuQuoin, my bride, Bessie Emling, and I opened a gift from Mom and Dad. Inside was the little bank, with five hundred dimes.

A handwritten note, which I still have, read:

The months and years have come and gone, dear Bob, since first this bank was given you. But as you'll find, its purpose still holds true. So please accept the contents, as a gift from your Mother and Dad, who wish for you and your wife a long, (useful) and happy life.

Left to my own devices, however, I could have made gobs of money as a boy. I didn't have to depend on 15¢ lawnmowing jobs. But when my big opportunity came knocking I was unable to grab it.

"Shorty" Strain, a little dried-up bachelor, was just what his nickname suggested—a ninety-pound bundle of business acumen. He owned an old trap of a car, a portable stand for selling snow cones, and two or three big glass jars. One weekend at the Williamson County Fairgrounds he gave me a job selling snow cones. My diary says I made 15¢—but that doesn't include all the snow cones I ate!

Every two or three hours, depending on business, we drove to the big ice plant near the C&EI station. Inside, we shoveled "snow"—the shavings left after the giant 500-pound slabs of ice were sawed into smaller pieces—into a washtub.

Just how sanitary that snow was by the time we had shaped it in the paper cups and squirted sweetened, colored water on it, I don't know. But it was a job, and a kid didn't make 15¢ every day—plus all the snow cones he wanted.

"Bob, how would you like to work for me all summer?" Shorty suggested. "We'll follow the fairs, carnivals, and races and have a big time. Also make you some spending money for school this fall."

I couldn't wait to tell Mom and Dad. Unfortunately, they didn't share my excitement. "Sleep in the back seat of old cars . . . live on hamburgers and snow cones . . . and mix with that carnival crowd?"

Well, I had tried. Some parents just don't appreciate their kids' desire to get out in the world and make a fortune before they're teenagers. So I settled for occasional sales to Two-Penny Louie.

ICE CREAM FOR BREAKFAST

The curtains hung limp at the windows in the four-room flat at 4415 St. Louis Avenue in St. Louis, where I was visiting my sister, Afton. Although it was only nine A.M., the heat of the July morning was already oppressive, and even the flies lacked the energy to buzz around the screen door.

"Bobby, what would you like for breakfast?" asked my fun-loving sister. "I'm hungry for ice cream. How about you?"

Now in Marion you didn't eat ice cream before noon, and scarcely before one or two in the afternoon. I had never even imagined ice cream for breakfast. It was beyond my wildest speculation.

Across the street was an ice cream parlor with row after row—hundreds, it seemed to me—of ice cream cabinets. And for only a nickel you could get a triple dip cone. They would even mix the flavors. The ice cream was piled so high that the clerks put tissue paper over the cones to keep the topmost dips from falling off.

In a few minutes I was picking my way, barefoot, across the hot bricks and streetcar rails of St. Louis Avenue, with four nickels jangling in my overalls—one for me, one for Afton, and one for each of her two boys, Frank, Jr. and Robert.

Who can put into words the delicacy of sitting in an airless flat, jammed so close to the neighbors you could almost read their newspapers, and gently licking a triple dip vanilla, chocolate, and strawberry cone for breakfast, while the sweat ran down your face?

Perish the heat. Damn the Depression. This was the city, 120 miles from Marion and a million miles from the WPA, relief orders, sour grapefruit, and sheep-lined winter coats that let the rain soak your pantlegs.

My first memory of St. Louis is of riding across Eads Bridge in my cousin Erby Hastings' cream-colored 1927 Chevrolet coupe. Dad and I rode in the rumble seat, and we delighted in the wind in our faces and the sight of the tall buildings as we bridged the Mississippi from East St. Louis.

But this time I had come by myself on the big, lumbering Greyhound bus that wound for nearly five hours through the small towns from Marion to St. Louis, making a rest stop at the Ashley Y, where everyone piled off for the restrooms and snacks. The round trip ticket had cost $1.60, so Mom had packed me a lunch, and I just walked around during the rest stop.

After high school, Afton took a short course at the old Brown's Business College in Marion. By the time she was sixteen, the shortage of jobs for young people had driven her to St. Louis, where she worked at the Brown Shoe Company. She was quick at the typewriter and other business machines, and her handwriting looked like the Palmer Method sample on the front cover of the dime tablets.

In St. Louis she married Frank Wolff. During the Depression he bought toilet soap at three bars for a dime and peddled it door-to-door for a nickel a bar. He also sold little ornamental paper butterflies which Afton made at home out of pastel-colored crepe paper and spring clothespins. Once Frank, Jr., was rushed to the hospital in a police emergency car after drinking one of the cans of gold paint which she used to make designs on the butterflies.

But the summer I visited them, the worst of the Depression was over. Frank worked two or three days a week at Nelson Manufacturing Company, making ice cream cabinets. In spring and early summer he sometimes worked five and six days a week.

And on top of all that luxury, he had converted an old ice box into a real electric refrigerator with the help of a used compressor. Since in Marion we cooled what little milk and butter we had in the well and carefully wrapped in a gunny sack the nickel's worth of ice we used sparingly for iced tea and lemonade, Frank's refrigerator was a marvel to me.

We had iced tea for lunch and iced tea for dinner and iced tea at bedtime. We kept one cube tray filled with koolaid, freezing homemade popsicles. And when you felt like it you could empty a tray of cubes just to hear them crack and splinter, or suck one in your mouth like candy.

An icemaker in the kitchen and a triple-dip ice cream store across the street! We were on top of the world. The Depression-ridden peddlers who pushed their carts up and down the streets, hollering at all hours, "Ice, ice for sale, ice for sale," could just go on by. They would need other customers to eke out their few dimes a day. We made our own ice!

Those two weeks in St. Louis represented everything we didn't have in Marion. St. Louis was big, it was brassy, and it was fun.

The day we went shopping downtown, Afton left me and my two nephews at the soda fountain in Woolworth's. She promised to be back by the time we finished our Cokes. But she wasn't. So Frank, Jr., and Robert, both only slightly younger than I, started inching their way down the long aisles of what was to me the biggest dime store in the world. I lit out in pursuit. I caught Robert first, put him back on the counter stool, and went back for Frank. By the time I lassoed him, Robert was gone again. In desperation, I caught both of them at once, pushed them down to the floor right in the middle of the store, and sat on them. Their screaming and struggling attracted the manager.

"Sonny, you're going to hurt those little boys. Why don't you let them up?"

I was too timid and overwhelmed to say anything. But I thought, "Mister, don't you know this is the biggest store in the world? You can't even see where the counters end. If I turned these boys loose they'd get so lost we'd never find them. And their mother told me to take care of them."

About the biggest Depression bargain in St. Louis was the weekend 25¢ pass on the streetcars and buses. If you had the endurance, you could ride non-stop from Saturday morning until midnight Sunday for a quarter. Which is almost what we did. We must have ridden hundreds of miles, from one end of the line to the other, crisscrossing the city from every angle. When the driver announced, "End of the line!" we'd hop off, cross the street, and catch the bus or streetcar going back. It was great!

The big air-conditioned movie palaces, with their gaudy lobbies, thick carpets, high ceilings, long balconies, and plaster-of-paris statuary, were almost as exciting as the movies themselves. Downtown we saw Dick Powell in *Singing Marine* at the Ambassador. And out on Grand Avenue, at the Fox Theater, we saw Warner Baxter, Wallace Beery, and Mickey Rooney in *Slave Ship*.

Another attraction on Grand Avenue on summer nights was Uncle Ben's Tent Revival. This St. Louis replica of Billy Sunday held forth summer after summer, with his integrated choir dressed in white shirts and blouses. But I'm afraid most people who attended went more for a free show than anything else.

One Sunday we went for an all-day trip down the Mississippi on the *S. S. President* (predecessor of the *Admiral*). Afton was up most of Saturday night pressing clothes and packing a big lunch basket. I was intrigued by the first miniature gherkin sweet pickles I had ever seen. My, they were sweet and juicy. But I couldn't understand why they had been picked so tiny. It would have seemed wasteful back in Marion to pick cucumbers that small. But lots of things were wasteful in Marion that were essential in St. Louis.

My cousin, Leo Casey, and his family met us at the wharf.

To everyone's horror, Leo discovered he had forgotten the tickets for his family. He jumped on the streetcar for a mad dash home. The whistle blew before he returned, and we had to board. I will never forget his family looking first at the boat, then back up the wharf to see if Leo would make it. Unfortunately, he didn't. As the boat eased away from shore, we saw Leo jump off the streetcar and run down to his wife and children. Too late.

"If I ever grow up and buy tickets for my family for the *S. S. President*," I said to myself, "I sure won't leave them lying on a dresser. I'll hold them in one hand in my pocket until I get to the boat."

I don't know how far downstream we sailed. Maybe eight miles. But as far as I was concerned, it might have been to New Orleans. It was a good day, and a long day, and the tiny pickles made the crunchiest sound when you bit off the end of one!

But the best was yet to come. On Friday night, payday, Frank kept the two boys and Afton and I went to Forest Park Highlands.

If there was a ride in that amusement park we didn't ride, I don't know what it was. We even rode the "mountain ride" (roller coaster) which threw me into mortal fear. It was dark when we boarded the little cars, and my wildest imagination could not have conceived tracks as steep or as high as those which soon unraveled ahead of us. I gave up all thought of living through the experience. The only question was whether we would die on this dip or the next.

We walked through the fun house, looking at ourselves in grotesque mirrors and watching the girls' dresses fly up when they stepped on the switch that triggered a giant fan under the floor. We ate hot dogs and drank red soda and won a kewpie doll by pressing a lever to bounce a tennis ball into a hopper.

Exhausted, we boarded a streetcar for St. Louis Avenue. After paying the fare, Afton opened her purse to count her money. Her face fell. The purse was empty.

"Bobby Jean," she said, using my full name as she did

when she wanted to make a point, "do you know what we've done? We've done gone and spent that whole $5 bill that Frank gave us. I mean we've spent every penny!"

Then, snapping her purse shut, she laughed as only a sister can laugh who has spent half a week's pay to light up the night with a thousand Roman candles for her kid brother from a coal-mining town in the Depression.

And believe it or not, I can still hear her laughing!

TOM MIX, HOOT GIBSON, AND RIN-TIN-TIN

Children reared with television cannot appreciate the magic world of adventure that came to life at the Saturday afternoon matinees in the thirties. A dime was the key that unlocked three wonderful hours of escape from the boarded-up businesses, the empty houses, and the silent mine tipples of a Depression-ridden Southern Illinois mining town.

Marion's first movie palace was commonly known as the Old Roland Theater, built by C. F. Roland. Regular showings stopped in 1925, but there were occasional movies until the Big Crash in 1929. I have faint memories of going there one time when it reopened for a special howing. One of the most successful films ever shown there was *The Birth of a Nation*. Scheduled for a week, it was all but rained out the first two nights when one of the worst electrical storms ever to hit Marion lasted for two days. The picture took in $1700 the rest of the week, however, an astronomical amount for those days, with many viewers coming from farms and the neighboring communities.

Show
Time
5:30

The Saturday afternoon shows I went to during the 30's were at the Orpheum Theater, built about 1930 on the southwest corner of the public square.

At one time during the Depression, admission for kids dropped to a nickel, with the use of a Kiddie Klub Kard. The attendant punched a hole in your card each Saturday, and when your card was punched out you got in free one Saturday. It was about the biggest Depression bargain in town.

For this amount you could see a couple of Mickey Mouse cartoons, previews of coming attractions—"Will it be another Western next Saturday or one of those silly love stories?"—a serial, and maybe a double feature.

If you had rounded up an extra nickel, you could stop at the Cline-Vick Drug Store before the show, sit at the marble counter, and order a twelve ounce bottle of Pepsi-Cola and a glass of crushed ice. One bottle would fill the smaller glasses four times, and, counting ice-sucking time, you had better allow at least fifteen minutes for this delectable ritual.

Or, in cold weather, you might stop at Woolworth's and use the nickel for a sack of chocolate-covered peanuts, lemon drops, chocolate kisses, toasted marshmallows, or peanut brittle. If you bought hard candy you could stretch a nickel sack for maybe an hour of movie time. Soft candy went faster, but even then you could prolong the ecstasy by completely chewing and swallowing one piece before starting on another.

The serials were twenty-minute segments of adventure movies, continued over twelve Saturdays. The purpose was to keep you coming back so as not to miss a single episode. The closing scene would be a stagecoach turning end over end down a cliff, carrying the heroine to possible death, while the hero thundered behind on his white horse. Or if the serial featured Rin-Tin-Tin, "the wonder dog," an episode might close with Rin-Tin-Tin jumping into an abandoned well to rescue one of the good guys.

Those were the days of Tom Mix, Hoot Gibson, Buck Jones, Gene Autry, and Hopalong Cassidy.

Also Spanky and Our Gang, Snow White, Joe E. Brown, W. C. Fields, the Marx Brothers, and Laurel and Hardy.

As well as Marie Dressler, Will Rogers, Shirley Temple, Clark Gable, Joan Crawford, Sonja Henie, Spencer Tracy, Wallace Beery, and Mae West.

Also Greta Garbo, Jean Harlow, William Powell, Dick Powell, Jane Withers, Robert Taylor, Myrna Loy, Errol Flynn, Jeannette McDonald and Nelson Eddy, James Cagney, and Gary Cooper.

Most of all we thrilled at the Westerns, with their long wagon trains, Indian wars, stampeding horses, runaway stagecoaches, fist fights, and prairie fires. The Old West, whether or not it remotely resembled what we saw on the screen, was real in our imaginations, for during the week we played out the drama of six-guns and wild ponies on State, Logan, and Glendale streets, which to us were the hills of Montana and the canyons of Wyoming.

And all for a dime—or just a nickel if you were a kard-karrying kiddie.

LUM AND ABNER

Whatever we paid for our first Atwater-Kent blue metal table-model radio, with its separate receiver and speaker, was worth the pleasure it brought during the Depression, if only to listen to *Lum and Abner* at six-thirty each week night.

Although Mom wasn't sure she could *ever* learn to operate the radio when a delivery truck from J. B. Heyde &

Sons brought it to 1404 N. State, she soon surprised herself by learning to use the knobs to find the stations and
control the volume. I can still hear her saying, "Now
Eldon, you and Bobby pay close attention to Mr. Heyde,
for I'll never learn to work all those buttons."

Lum and Abner, originating in the mythical Jot-'Em-
Down Store in Pine Ridge, Arkansas, brought such a
hometown folksiness into our living room that we felt the
characters were real company. It was pure corn and
nostalgia, but the program dulled the cutting edge of the
Depression in untold numbers of homes such as ours.

Cedric Wehunt, Grandpappy Spears, and Squire Skimp were just about as real as Lum Edwards and Abner Peabody themselves. When the party line rang in Pine Ridge, everyone listened, the people in Marion and a thousand other such communities all over the nation.

Television was unknown to the public and movies charged admission. But after supper, all over America, families sat back to a marvelous, manufactured world in which you supplied the pictures while the radio brought in the sound.

There was the NBC Red network and the NBC Blue network, as well as CBS and MBS. Our favorite stations included nearby WEBQ in Harrisburg, KMOX in St. Louis, WLS in Chicago, and WSM in Nashville. We occasionally pulled in XERX, "the world's most powerful radio station" from Del Rio, Texas, where temperance leader Sam Morris warned that "liquor sold in a pretty bottle with a government tax stamp on it will make a man just as drunk and just as brutal to his wife as bootleg whiskey sold in a fruit jar in a back alley."

When Smiling Ed McConnell sang and described the Aladdin "magic" lamp, he made everyone with electric lights wish he were living in the country so he could buy one of those kerosene lights that were so easy on the kids' eyes and so hard on rural darkness.

Offering such premiums as a shooting plane, hovering disc, gun, and secret whistle code, *Jack Armstrong, the "All-American Boy,"* came on at five-fifteen with the theme from the "Hudson High Fight Song":

> Won't you try Wheaties?
> They're whole wheat with all the bran.
> Won't you try Wheaties?
> For wheat is the best food of man.
> . . . with sugar and cream they're just fine.

At five-thirty Ovaltine sponsored *Little Orphan Annie* (Leapin' lizards!) with her free offers of bracelets, secret codes, shake-up mugs, rings, buttons, and badges:

> Who's that little chatterbox?
> The one with pretty auburn locks?
> Who do you see?
> It's Little Orphan Annie . . .

At five forty-five Pepsodent toothpaste brought Lowell Thomas with the evening news ("Hello, everybody!"), still going strong in 1971. Since we didn't take a paper in the Depression, it was Lowell Thomas who brought the world into our little neighborhood. And when he signed off on Friday night, "So long until Monday," we felt lonely because it would be three days before we again caught up with the world through Lowell Thomas.

In 1931 he announced the death of Notre Dame football coach Knute Rockne in a plane crash near Bazaar, Kansas. In 1932 he described the World War I veterans' march on Washington, demanding their bonus in full.

In 1933 he told us that Adolph Hitler was now Chancellor of Germany, and that the German Reichstag building in Berlin had been destroyed by fire, probably set by the Nazis. The same year he announced that Prohibition had been repealed when Utah ratified the twenty-first Amendment to the Constitution, the thirty-sixth state to do so.

Then in 1934 Lowell Thomas described the shooting of gangster John Dillinger by FBI men outside a Chicago movie house, and the birth of the Dionne sisters, first quintuplets to survive beyond infancy.

In 1935 Thomas announced the death of comedian Will Rogers and pilot Wiley Post in an air crash near Point Barrow, Alaska.

The Duke of Windsor captured much of the news in 1936 when he gave up the throne of England for "the woman I love," Mrs. Wallis Warfield Simpson, a divorcee from Baltimore.

In 1937, Lowell Thomas announced the tragic death of yet another national figure, Amelia Earhart, near the Howland Islands in the Pacific, and also the sinking of the United States gunboat Panay by Japanese shells on the Yangtze River.

One of the most bizarre events of 1937 was the journey of "Wrong Way Corrigan," who flew across the Atlantic from New York to Dublin, with neither permit or passport, claiming he thought he was flying to Los Angeles.

Perhaps the most significant news of 1938 which Thomas shared, the importance of which was not recognized at the time, was the conference in Munich at which Britain and France yielded to Nazi demands for the cession of the Sudetenland to Germany by Czechoslovakia.

After the news we tuned in *Amos and Andy*, a top network show of the thirties, which continued five nights a week until as late as 1960. When Freeman Gosden and Charles Correll came on the NBC Red network at six o'clock CST, playing the roles of two black men in Harlem, telephone use all over the country dropped by fifty percent. Many movie theaters even shut off their projectors to pipe in *Amos and Andy*, and some thirty million listeners tuned them in, including President Roosevelt. Kingfish was the top man in their fictitious lodge, the Mystic Knights of the Sea. Lightnin' was clean-up man at the lodge, and Amos operated the Fresh Air Taxi Company. Other characters included Brother Crawford, Madam Queen, and Miss Blue ("Buzz me, Miss Blue . . .").

On Monday nights you could listen to Eddie Cantor, George Burns and Gracie Allen, and Wayne King's orchestra. Tuesday night brought *Big Town* with Edward G. Robinson, *Fibber McGee and Molly*, and Al Jolson.

Wednesay night you could dial *One Man's Family* and *Town Hall Tonight*. Thursday brought Rudy Vallee, Major Bowes' *Amateur Hour* ("The wheel of fortune goes round and round, and where she stops, nobody knows.") and Kate Smith with Ted Collins ("When the Moon Comes over the Mountain").

Death Valley Days, with its creaking wagon wheels, and Paul Whiteman's orchestra, came on Friday. And of course Saturday night brought the perennial favorite, the *Grand Ol' Opry* from Nashville, Tennessee.

If you sat up late enough, H. V. Kaltenborn would also bring the news, but we settled for Lowell Thomas at six P.M.

There were others, such as *Helen Trent*, the daytime heroine of soap opera, *The Lone Ranger*, with his speedy steed—"Hi-O Silver!"—and the *Junior G-Men*, offering a real G-Man badge for a Post Toasties box top and 25¢. It was an unfolding panorama which you saw with your ears and felt in your heart—American radio in the bottomed-out Thirties.

SHADY REST

Halfway between Marion and Harrisburg was a cabin known sometimes as "The Hut" but more often as "Shady Rest." It figured prominently in the Birger-Shelton gang wars of the 1920's in Franklin and Williamson counties. Built in 1924, it sat about a hundred yards north of Route 13 in a thick grove of trees.

By way of amusement it offered not only bootleg liquor and gambling but also cockfights and dog fights. Liquor

runners from Florida were said to lay over there during
the day, making the last leg of the trip to St. Louis after
dark. Though it was notorious throughout Southern Illinois, it was never molested by the authorities.

"When I used to drive from Marion to Harrisburg,"
my cousin Erby Hastings recalls, "I always speeded up
when I passed Shady Rest. I didn't look to the right or
the left."

Its foot-thick logs walls were practically bulletproof,
and the deep basement afforded safety during an attack.
Rifles, submachine guns, and boxes of ammunition, plus
stores of canned goods, lined the walls. Floodlights, pow-
ered by a generator on the grounds, prevented surprise
attacks after dark.

Here was the hideout of Charlie Birger, the archrival
of the Shelton gang, and the last man legally hanged in
Illinois, which event took place at Benton on April 19,
1928. Charlie was convicted of the murder of Mayor Joe
Adams of West City and of taking part in the murder of
Patrolman and Mrs. Lory Price.

Believe it or not, Shady Rest was the target of some
homemade bombs dropped from an airplane on November 10, 1926. On January 9, 1927, Birger's enemies were
more successful. Shady Rest was burned to the ground,
and four unidentifiable skeletons were found in the black-
ened ruins.

When I was a boy, the very name "Shady Rest" put
terror into my heart. Each time we passed the site someone would point out the location of the burned cabin, and
we would imagine gangsters with machine guns hiding
behind the big trees.

Evidently, cockfighting continued intermittently near
the burned-out cabin. One afternoon Dad and I were
passing Shady Rest and, on an impulse, we stopped. In a
clearing a group of men, preparing for a cockfight, were
making their wagers.

They armed a white cock and a red cock with sharp, deadly spurs on their ankles. Then they turned them loose. Around and around in circles they hopped, jabbing and thrusting and retreating.

Then the spur of the red-feathered cock found its mark in the neck of its rival, whose white wings slowly turned crimson from its own blood.

We soon left. Each summer we always raised a few chickens, for which Dad pulled grass, drew fresh water in the hot weather, warmed water in winter—they were almost pets to him. They were also a welcome source of eggs and meat.

The crimson-spotted, gasping white cock lying in the dust seemed to symbolize the senseless killing and lawlessness of the twenties, and I was glad when we pulled out onto Route 13 and headed west toward Marion.

A   FIGHT   ON   THE   SQUARE

Men around Marion had a lot of spare time during the Depression, and much of it was spent on the public square talking politics and trading knives. At one time a stone ledge surrounded the Williamson County Courthouse, a favorite loafing place where men could sit and whittle in the sun. If President Roosevelt had just known the wisdom that was going to waste on that square, he would have made a personal trip to Marion for a solution to the nation's economic ills.

Dad often described the public square as he remembered it from his young manhood—unpaved street with hogs "wallerin' " in the mud, and board sidewalks.

Dad enjoyed standing around the square, meeting his friends and talking—another favorite spot was the hitchrack northeast of the square. Saturday afternoon would

nearly always find him uptown, and invariably he would
stop at Woolworth's and buy a nickel or dime's worth of
chocolate covered peanuts.

Somehow, Saturday night is intertwined in my memory with a white sack of chocolate covered peanuts, and
if I ever get lonesome or bored, even on a trip, I'll pull
up at a dime store and buy a sack of chocolate covered
peanuts. Then I feel very close to Dad and my boyhood.

One day, during the Depression, he and my Uncle
Charley Anderson got into an argument on the square.
I don't know what over, but probably not politics, since
both were Republicans. The argument heated up, and
before either knew what was happening, they got into a
fight. How much of a fight I don't know. I'm sure the re-
ports were greatly exaggerated. Maybe one merely
pushed the other. Anyway, the "fight" broke up real
quick, but the hard feelings lasted for weeks.

We didn't visit the Andersons. The Andersons didn't
visit us. Mom and Aunt Bertha even got involved in a
letter-writing exchange. My brother LaVerne served as

courier for the letters, as each was hesitant to send her missives through the mail. When he announced one day that he had carried his last letter, the letter writing stopped.

Then one day there was a reconciliation, brought about by my Uncle Marshall and Aunt Alverta. They were to be at Aunt Bertha's for dinner, and they insisted we come. Which we did, amidst a great deal of hugging and crying and handshaking.

"You two grown men ought to be ashamed of yourselves," Uncle Marshall lectured. "Fighting like little boys, and right up there on the public square where everyone could see you."

Looking back, I am sure the fight is greatly overrated in my memory. Maybe I exaggerated it at the time because I got a certain boyish pride out of the fact that Dad had a public fight "right up town where everybody could see you."

Why? Because in Williamson County, from 1868 through 1927, men often took matters into their own hands and tried to solve problems with force. There were four distinct eras of violence. First was the bloody vendetta of 1868–76, when at least six men died as the result of a family feud between four prominent county families —the Crains, Bulliners, Hendersons, and Sisneys.

Second was the Herrin Massacre of 1922, which climaxed a reign of terror between union and non-union miners that started in 1890.

Third was the Ku Klux Klan era, 1923–26, when thousands of Southern Illinoisans took "law and order" into their own hands to fight the bootleggers, gamblers, and those who merchandised prostitution.

Fourth was the inter-gang war of 1926–27 between the Sheltons and the Birgers over the control of liquor and gambling.

Any boy tends to identify with the lore of his boyhood home. If the Depression blues were lightened by a family feud, who was to deny a boy his adventuresome dreams, even if the "fight" was no more than a shoving contest over how many little pigs President Roosevelt had drowned in the Mississippi River?

THE SALESMAN

Jacob and Sarah Bradley Gordon, my maternal grandparents, moved to Marion about 1907 from a farm in Johnson County. About 1914, Mr. Gordon and Dad opened a neighborhood grocery at 511 East Boulevard.

In his later years, when he returned to Johnson County, Grandpa Gordon operated a country grocery in a sort of makeshift shed near his home.

In both stores he displayed a hand-lettered sign, made on plain cardboard. It read exactly like this:

> Since man to man is so unjust,
> I do not no what man to trust;
> I've trusted often to my sorrow,
> So pay today and I'll trust tomorrow.

Erby Hastings, my cousin, remembers working for Dad and Grandpa in the store on East Boulevard when he was a teenager. "Each morning I would go door to door, taking orders," he recalls. "Later I would deliver the orders in a buggy. Competition was real, and you had to get out early or someone would beat you to the business."

In the 1920's, Dad built a new neighborhood grocery store next to our home on North State. It was eventually closed by the Depression and the chain stores.

When the Depression hit, my dad had some background as a salesman. To this he turned much of his energy. He started out selling iron cords from door to door, but nobody was buying iron cords. If anything, they were digging out their old cordless flatirons, which they heated on the cook stove.

One summer Dad tried selling Bibles door to door, but with little success. I went along with him for a few days, working mainly in Johnston City. I think I may have sold one Bible.

His most successful venture, near the end of the Depression, was selling coal up around Salem and Kinmundy in south central Illinois. He started very modestly. He found a trucker who would pay him 25¢ for every ton he could sell.

About the middle of one summer, he and a trucker by the name of Al Shackelford left early one morning for Salem. Al parked on a residential street, and Dad went door to door until he found someone with enough money to buy his winter's supply of coal in July. And believe me, that wasn't easy!

But he kept at it until November. If he sold a five-ton load, that was $1.25. Out of this he would buy his lunch, if he hadn't taken lunch from home. The transportation was free, as he rode in the truck.

He kept a record of each customer in a nickel tablet from Woolworth's. The next summer he wrote a postcard to each one, reminding them he would soon be by. Over three or four summers he developed quite a list of regular customers. At one time, two or three trucks were hauling coal for him. This doubled and tripled his commissions.

Often a customer would write, "Mr. Hastings, I want another load of coal, the same as you brought me last summer."

He tried to remember what kind of coal best fitted the customer's needs—whether the coal was for a stoker, a hand-fired furnace, a heating stove, or an open grate. He also carried along a broom, and after the coal was unloaded he went back and swept up any that had fallen on the sidewalk or lawn. His customers appreciated his care, and the success they brought him was the opening wedge in the late 30's that brought us through the Depression.

Sometimes I went along, and I felt very grown up riding in the cab of those old trucks, bouncing along for three or four hours up twisting Route 37, now paralleled by wide, modern, straight Interstate 57.

He and the driver often left as early as four A.M. and got home after dark. It was a long ride, and a long day, but a long way from the WPA.

The night before, if Al were already loaded, he might pull up in our driveway to talk with Dad about where they were going and when they would leave. I would look at Al's huge truck, sagging under the big, black lumps of Williamson County coal. In the gathering dusk, the chunks of coal looked like chunks of gold.

A $1.67 BIBLE FROM SEARS

Both Dad's and Mom's families had Baptist backgrounds. Dad's father, John Hise Hastings, and Uncle William came from near Paris, Tennessee to Southern Illinois about the time of the outbreak of the Civil War. Evidently the two teenagers came alone, perhaps looking for a chance to enlist in the Union army, which they both did; they were participants in Sherman's march to the sea.

After the war John married Edie Groves, and they settled about six miles east of Marion, near Pulley's Mill, and attended Davis Prairie Church, one of the earliest Baptist congregations in Williamson County. Edie was baptized there in 1871.

Dad often told me about the big summer revivals at Davis Prairie Church, which still stands on Route 13 east of Marion. "The roads were impassable in the winter, and we didn't go anywhere until spring. So churchgoing was saved for the summer. We had big crowds, and I can remember people standing outside, crowding around the windows, trying to see and hear."

But the camp meetings or "brush arbor" revivals drew the biggest crowds. "When a meeting opened, we always knew there would be one mourner, Uncle Pratus Groves," Dad told me. "He would come forward during the invitation, get down on his knees, even lie down in the straw. No amount of praying or exhorting would help him make a profession. He would stay as late as anyone would pray with him. Finally some men would load him bodily in the wagon and take him home. The next night it would be the same. Every night of the revival, the same. And again the next summer. I don't know how long this went on— maybe for years. Finally Uncle Pratus 'got religion.' And when he did, he said, 'You know, all that prayin' weren't necessary. I just never got humble enough to let the Lord have his way.' "

Baptists were the first non-Catholics to found a church in Illinois. It was formed at New Design, near the present town of Waterloo, in 1796. But Baptists were slow to organize in the little village of Marion. In 1865 nine members from Davis Prairie Church joined with ten other residents to found the First Baptist Church.

When Grandpa and Grandma Gordon moved to Marion, about 1907, Mom started going to First Baptist, where she was converted and baptized as a young girl. After they were married, Dad was also baptized there.

My first memories of churchgoing are not from Sunday School, but from Sunday night services. Big crowds, as many as a thousand persons, attended the night services at First Baptist during the 20's. The large attendance was partly due to the pulpit power of pastor A. E. Prince and partly to the church's involvement in the Prohibition lawlessness.

The rivalry between the Birger and Shelton gangs for the control of bootlegging, gambling, and prostitution helped give "Bloody Williamson" its nickname. First Baptist Church was caught in the struggle. Pastor Prince kept two revolvers, one in his car and one in his desk at the church.

On April 6, 1924, the Ku Klux Klan, wearing the traditional hoods, marched down the aisle at the evening service, knelt at the altar, left an offering, and then marched out.

In February, 1927, the funeral of state highway patrolman Lory L. Price was held at First Baptist. Price and his wife had been killed by one of the warring gangs. Every available seat was filled for the funeral, and hundreds of people stood outside in the streets. Machine guns were mounted at all four corners of the church roof, for fear the gang that had done the killing might cause trouble. Mom described this funeral so often that I am uncertain whether I was actually present or just felt I had been because of her frequent retellings.

About four-thirty on the morning of April 20, 1927, the front of the church was bombed, after it had been announced that a number of "dry" candidates had won an election. Most of the "dries" were members of First Baptist.

So there was a certain drama about the big Sunday evening crowds of the twenties, and we usually arrived early for a good seat, often accompanied by Aunt Bertha Anderson. I know she went with us, because she always gave me a stick of Teaberry chewing gum to help pass the time until services began.

The most lasting influence of First Baptist on my life began the Christmas I got a $1.67 Bible from Sears Roebuck. (I know the cost because I looked it up in the catalog!) This was a red letter edition, the words of Christ being printed in red.

That same year we studied the life of Christ in Sunday School. For the first time, I read the Bible seriously, especially the four Gospels.

I was particularly impressed with what Jesus taught about the worth of a human being. I saw that people are more important than things, and that a man might gain the whole world and still lose his soul—his own true being and personality. I was impressed with the knowledge that a man's life does not consist in the abundance of the things which he possesses.

These teachings, against the backdrop of the Great Depression, had heightened significance for me. They helped me to see that true happiness is not dependent on material things; that you can be poor and still rich emotionally at the same time.

In the parables of the lost sheep, the lost coin, and the lost boy I saw just how important one person is in God's sight.

Looking back, I realize that this is where I received my values for life. You might have to stand in line on Saturday for a nickel's worth of skim milk, but neither skim milk nor whole milk nor buttermilk nor surplus powdered milk had anything to do with a man's real worth.

Not that food and housing and education were unimportant. But that something else and someone else mattered more. He was God, and his revelation in human form was Jesus Christ.

So, on my profession of that faith, I was baptized on Easter Sunday night of 1935 in the church where the Ku Klux Klan had paraded, the bombs had exploded, and the machine guns had guarded a funeral.

Fortunately, First Baptist was a happy meeting ground for persons of various backgrounds during the Depression. Here I met and made friends with people who had jobs and steady incomes but were still kind and friendly to those with less. It was as if we were standing before the cross, where the ground is always level.

In this respect, I remember Mr. and Mrs. Ed Alexander, who owned Alexander's Dry Goods Store on the public square. I was impressed to find that these successful, well-dressed business people were so faithful and friendly, standing at the door on Sunday mornings passing out bulletins and greeting newcomers.

The Alexanders lived in a big house at 815 N. Market, with a beautiful lawn where they entertained Mom's T. E. L. Sunday School class each August. It was always a gala affair, with Japanese lanterns and all the works. Mom looked forward to it for months, and, like Cinderella, talked about it for months afterwards.

If Dad and I were to walk her home through the dark, we would arrive a few minutes early and, waiting across the street in the shadows, stand in awe of the soft light and the laughter which drifted across the way, almost wishing that we, too, had been invited.

A WHITE SUIT FOR GRADUATION

I graduated from the eighth grade on June 3, 1938, after finishing junior high at the old Washington School on West Jefferson. It was built in 1886 and torn down in 1968 to make room for the present Williamson County Courthouse.

Dad completed only the fifth grade, but he remembers visiting Washington School one day while his sister Annie was a pupil there, probably about 1888. Mom completed the eighth grade, also at Washington, and my two brothers and sister went there, too.

The first school on that site was built of logs cut in the Crab Orchard Creek bottoms. During a wet winter, when the building was new, the logs would sprout, affording the teacher a constant supply of switches with which to enforce discipline.

On the night before graduation I attended a party for eighth graders at the Boy Scout cabin in southeast Marion, and walked part of the way home with Philip B. Harris. Phil had first taught me that a noun "is a person, place or thing" in sixth-grade English at Logan School. Later, when I was at Washington School, he was a teacher and basketball coach.

It was a warm summer night, and we walked up South Market to the square, then around it, and then north on North Market.

"Bob," he asked, "have you ever thought what you want to do in life?"

I swallowed hard. No one had ever asked me that.

"Yes," I answered hesitantly. "I thought I might someday be a preacher . . ."

We continued to the corner of Boulevard and North Market where he turned left and I headed straight for East DeYoung, then on to State. It was nearly midnight, and it seemed an awfully long way from the street light at Market and DeYoung to the light at DeYoung and State, and still further up State until I could see our porch light with its tiny 40-watt bulb.

I turned into the walk at our yard, past the maple tree I had climbed in the spring of 1934, to fasten a ring from a looseleaf notebook on one of the limbs, and had climbed again on June 7, 1937, to carve my initials on the same limb, pointing to the now-imbedded ring—a valueless secret known only to me.

Inside, I undressed in the dark.

"Is that you, Bob?" Mom asked from her bedroom.

"Yes."

"Did you have a good time?"

"Yes."

"Did you walk home with Phil?"

"Yes."

"Remember the porch light."

"OK."

I slipped into bed, rolled over next to the window, and for a long time looked at the stars through the screen.

For graduation the next day I wore my first suit, a white one. And a white shirt with a navy blue tie and matching handkerchief and white shoes.

After the ceremonies at the Orpheum Theatre, we stopped at Kroger's on north Market to buy our week's groceries. Before much longer the old-style counters would be gone—the ones where you lined up for a clerk to "wait on" you. But this time a clerk did wait on us, going to the shelves for each item as we called it off.

Then, picking up the sacks of groceries in our arms, we began the one-mile walk out North Market and up North State to 1404.

It was a beautiful afternoon, with white puffy clouds dotting the blue sky. We walked with light, confident steps. In another year both Mom and Dad would have jobs with steady, if small, incomes. In another year we would have a telephone—468-R—and the next year a secondhand car. Then on May 22, 1939, we would go to the Marion Water Department and make a $4 deposit to turn the water back on, after workmen had dug a deep, ten-inch sewer line through our yard for the indoor bathroom.

That fall, before I started to high school, there would be a new green wool coat—we called them bush jackets —belted at the back and with six buttons down the front. It would keep me dry and warm.

And to top everything off, I had just learned that at Southern Illinois Normal University, only seventeen miles away, anyone could work enough to pay his way through college.

The skim milk and the nickel's worth of ice and the sheep-lined coat and the eight-year speller and the WPA and the sour grapefruit were now history. There were no storm clouds on my horizon . . .

Epilogue

FOR THIRTY-ONE more summers Mom would can Elberta peaches that had ripened on the gently sloping hills of Southern Illinois. And make grape and blackberry jelly. And each fall "speak for" a bushel of sweet potatoes, a gallon of sorghum, a peck of winesap apples.

For twenty-one more years Mom and Dad would call 1404 N. State their home. For twenty-one more Valentine Days Dad would plant his neighborhood-famous lettuce bed. Then in 1959 they moved to 206 N. Liberty, near downtown Marion, where they could walk to church, the grocery, and their doctor.

Dad passed away in 1968, and Mom in 1970. After Mom's death, while clearing out her kitchen shelves, I found her last two quarts of home-canned peaches. A wave of nostalgia quenched my appetite, and I gave them to her thoughtful neighbor, Mrs. Ina Etherton.

Anyone who has disposed of his parents' effects knows the emotion. What got next to me were the few remaining relics of the Depression—a colander, the old-time heating irons, a scrub board, the "foot tub" in which Mom washed LaVerne's feet in 1936, the old barbering tools Dad had used to cut the neighborhood kids' hair, a last for repairing shoe soles, and a garden hoe with half the handle missing, filed down to almost nothing. Some might have called it junk. But to me these were the banners of our struggle, the aging weapons of our battle with poverty.

The Depression died slowly in Southern Illinois. When I entered the small teachers' college at Carbondale in the fall of 1942, the scars were still visible. The Baptists of Illinois had purchased a white, two-story frame house at 313 W. Grand to rent to boys. When it opened, its cooking facilities could best be described as primitive. An early resident tells how for a few days one fall the boys cooked over an open fire in the yard.

I know this sounds unbelievable for the forties. But it is a true, if isolated, incident. When I went home on weekends, Mom would send me back with five oranges and five boiled eggs, which would keep until Friday without refrigeration. This was breakfast for five mornings.

Yet I never felt deprived. I was so elated over attending Southern Illinois Normal University that any sacrifice seemed trivial.

I enrolled at S.I.N.U. for two reasons. First, the school of only a few hundred students was near home and ridiculously inexpensive. Second, it was about the only college I knew anything about. Honestly. No high-school counselor so much as suggested writing for other university catalogs (there were no counselors). No one from my family had ever attended college. It was an unexplored world.

But I had been to band contests on the Carbondale campus, and I knew a few young people who had commuted to Carbondale on the old Courtney Bus Line.

So it was a matter of getting up one morning and showing up on campus. No preregistration, no advisement, no offers of student aid. Just fill out your registration cards in the Old Gym and start to class.

As the college mushroomed after World War II and merited a change of name to Southern Illinois University, I continued to be impressed with one thing—the concern of the University for neighboring counties. The school was committed to area development, to making Southern Illinois a better place to live.

If what I've said leaves the impression that a certain isolationism existed in Southern Illinois in the thirties, it is a correct impression. For the people who grew up there, including my own family, there was an isolation, an aloofness, as surely as if the area had been ringed with the mountains of Appalachia. Southern Illinois University was a gap in those mountains.

Those who experienced the Depression often say, "Today's kids have it too easy. They would be better off with a few of those hardships."

I don't necessarily agree. The Depression was a struggle for survival, and any struggle leaves its marks. The Depression marked me, and I'm not certain the marks were all good. At one time, as a college student, I held three part-time jobs. Making money to pay bills often came before study and extracurricular activities. Was that altogether good?

We can't impose yesterday on today. Each generation has its own problems. Learning to cope with material prosperity may be just as challenging as surviving a Depression.

Successful living involves an attitude, a spirit, a set of values—whatever you want to call it. Each person must find meaning in life as he copes with the unique problems of his generation. We cannot artificially impose yesterday's problems on today's society and expect instant happiness. This is a simplistic wish for panaceas that fizzles in the arena of reality.

What a youngster's feet touch as he jumps out of bed —cold linoleum or warm carpeting—does not necessarily mark his destiny. What counts is the kind of person who walks across these floors. We must never forget this. Because what we are and who we are is far more than what we eat or where we live or what we wear.

If you have read this far you know that I am a sentimentalist. Unashamedly and unapologetically so. I cried before I wrote this. I cried as I wrote it. And I still cry when I read it. Which may explain what I am about to say.

In the summer of 1971 I took one of my daughters to a large campus for orientation and Parents' Day. We stayed in one of the campus residences, a move designed to give prospective students a sampling of dormitory life and food.

What got next to me were the available drinks. There were whole milk, skim milk, chocolate milk, hot chocolate, coffee, iced tea, hot tea, grapeade, and four choices of soft drinks. I believe that adds up to twelve. Some boys took three glasses of milk at a time. They could go back as often as they wished, with no additional charge over the basic fees.

Some enterprising soul on this campus was really pushing mini-refrigerators for rent to students. After all, if you have only twelve choices of drinks, and that just three times a day, you need supplementary, instant refreshment in your room!

I blinked back two big tears. Honestly I did. I couldn't help it. And I was too embarrassed to use a handkerchief. For I saw the lonely pint of milk on the supper table in Marion, the line of customers at the Marion City Dairy, and the orange-and-boiled-egg breakfasts at Carbondale.

"Gee," I thought, "there ought to be some happy medium in all this, what with kids starving in Pakistan and all that."

Now, to use a Southern Illinois colloquialism, I've done gone and said more than I should've.

I just wanted to say that when I was ten, I came home one day with a big bucket of skim milk, topped with a thin skiff of ice, and boy, it sure was good . . .